SAINTS FOR HEALING

SAINTS *for* HEALING

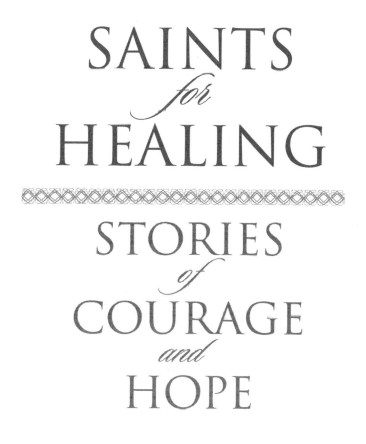

STORIES *of* COURAGE *and* HOPE

JANICE McGRANE, S.S.J.

ST. ANTHONY MESSENGER PRESS
Cincinnati, Ohio

Scripture passages have been taken from *New Revised Standard Version Bible,*
copyright ©1989 by the Division of Christian Education of the National Council of
the Churches of Christ in the U.S.A., and used by permission. All rights reserved.

Cover and book design by Mark Sullivan

ISBN 978-0-86716-962-1

LIBRARY OF CONGRESS CATALOGING-IN-PUBLICATION DATA
McGrane, Janice, 1949-
Saints for healing: stories of courage and hope / Janice McGrane.
p. cm.
Includes bibliographical references (p.).
ISBN 978-0-86716-962-1 (alk. paper)
1. Christian saints—Biography. 2. Catholic Church—Clergy—Biography. 3. Healing—
Religious aspects—Catholic Church—Meditations. I. Title.
BX4655.3.M34 2011
282.092'2—dc22
[B]
2010051491

Published by St. Anthony Messenger Press
28 W. Liberty St.
Cincinnati, OH 45202
www.SAMPBooks.org
www.AmericanCatholic.org

Printed in the United States of America.
Printed on acid-free paper.
11 12 13 14 15 5 4 3 2 1

For my mother, Trudy, and my sister, Joan,
whose loving embrace made this book possible.

CONTENTS

Acknowledgments . . . . *ix*

Introduction . . . . *xi*

Note to Readers . . . . *xv*

Chapter One: Hildegard of Bingen (1098–1179)

      Healing and Visions 1

Chapter Two: St. Catherine of Siena (1347–1380)

      Healing the Church 13

Chapter Three: St. Joan of Arc (1412–1431)

      Healing France While Hearing Voices 27

Chapter Four: Venerable Henriette Delille (1812–1862)

      Healing the Slaves of New Orleans 41

Chapter Five: St. Damien of Molokai (1840–1889)

      Healing the Untouchables of Molokai 53

Chapter Six: St. Edith Stein (1891–1942) and

      St. Maximilian Kolbe (1894–1941)

      Healing During the Agony of Auschwitz . . . 69

Chapter Seven: Dorothy Day (1897–1980)

      Healing God's Working Poor 87

Chapter Eight: Blessed Mother Teresa of Calcutta (1910–1997)

      Healing in the Slums of Calcutta 99

Chapter Nine: Archbishop Oscar Romero (1917–1980)

      Healing El Salvador 109

Chapter Ten: Fr. Mychal Judge (1933–2001)

      Healing with Heroism 123

Notes 133

Bibliography 139

ACKNOWLEDGMENTS

With gratitude to my loyal editors, Sisters of St. Joseph Kathleen Rooney, Marion Aherne, Adrienne Bucci, and Joan Riethmiller, and especially to my indefatigable copying expert, Sr. Assunta Bonner.

Special thanks to Sr. Marie Clare Kleschick, S.S.J., for introducing me to Henriette Delille; Sr. Normandie Gaitley, for assistance with Edith Stein; and Sr. Anastasia Hearne, S.S.J., for sharing her friendship with Mother Teresa.

I also thank: Sr. Sylvia Thibodeaux, S.S.F., and Sr. Doris Godeaux, S.S.F.; Ken Bradley, Kathleen Lunn, Teresa Naughton, Fr. John McKenzie, Harry Tucker, Dolores Smith, Bob and Carol Jensen, Celeste Robinson, and Joyce Dutill.

I'd also like to thank the following for their hospitality: the Benedictine Sisters of St. Gertrude Monastery, Ridgely, Maryland; Sr. Nadine Boyle, R.S.M.; Sisters of the Holy Family of New Orleans; and Margo Casey.

Finally, with gratitude to the following Sisters of St. Joseph: Mary Elizabeth Clark, Eileen Side, Ann Edgar Hess, Catherine Looker, Mary Fineran, St. Ursula Egan, Kathy McMenamin, and Eileen Lynch.

INTRODUCTION

I have been surprised and gratified at the response to my first book, *Saints to Lean On: Spiritual Companions for Illness and Disability*. In our secular age, it is clear that people still have a deep thirst for spiritual companionship, especially during difficult times. It can help to know that holy people have walked a similar path and would like to offer us spiritual comfort.

While the theme of *Saints to Lean On* was about how various members of the communion of saints coped with their illness or disability (or both), the focus of this second book is on healing. I would like to make it clear that I am using "healing" in a broad sense, certainly including physical healing, but also other types of healing experiences. The community prayer of my religious congregation, the Sisters of St. Joseph of Philadelphia, invites us to be a healing presence in any and all situations. A smile, an expression of affection, a conversation, or simply "being there" for another person can all be healing experiences.

Healing also occurs on a larger scale: Joan of Arc healed the morale of France in its most dire hour; Edith Stein and Maximilian Kolbe offered comfort and consolation in the midst of the horror of Auschwitz; Henriette Delille transcended the insidious racism of her time to minister with slaves; and Hildegard of Bingen's knowledge of healing herbs has lasted through the ages. It is my hope that their stories, along with those of the other saints in this book, will invite readers to turn to them for companionship and inspiration in times of their own need for healing.

I also would like to address the question of suffering. Suffering is not a popular concept in the world of disability activists, for good reason. One, a person with a disability is not necessarily suffering, and most likely is living a happy and productive life. Only *you*, no one else, can decide when you are genuinely suffering. Sometimes I wonder if people are projecting onto me how *they* would feel if they had my disability. What they don't see is the sustaining grace with which God has blessed me. Each of us receives the grace to live our own lives, not someone else's.

A second reason for our lack of enthusiasm regarding the suffering label is that it tends to distance us from other people. In a society that abhors suffering, those of us with disabilities simply do not want the mantle of suffering placed on us. We need to be related to as people, with the same virtues and vices everyone else has.

This is not to deny that human suffering certainly exists. All people are touched by it, in some way, at some time in their lives. This, again, is where our faith comes in. Nowhere in Scripture are we promised an easy life. At the end of Matthew's Gospel, Jesus assures us that he will be with us. He does not promise that our lives will be easy but he does assure us that he will walk with us intimately.

Each of the individuals in this book knew this. They were convinced down to their bones that Jesus accompanied them always— whether in a Carmelite cloister, nineteenth-century New Orleans, or the slums of Calcutta. A deep relationship with Jesus was their secret way of coping with their particular hardships.

As "wounded healers," Hildegard of Bingen lived with a painful chronic condition, Maximilian Kolbe was rejected for his ideas by his fellow priests, Mother Teresa lived in deep spiritual darkness for most of her life, and yet they all knew that suffering made them stronger. As Kahlil Gibran is oft quoted, "Out of suffering emerge the strongest souls...the mightiest characters have the greatest scars." We can ask God to let our own scars connect us to the scars of the "mighty characters" in these pages.

It is my hope then, that readers of this book become wounded healers themselves. May the hope and joy, strength and courage in these pages inspire you to be a healing presence to the people in your life.

One of the statements that received the most response in *Saints to Lean On: Spiritual Companions for Illness and Disability* is the fact that we pray *with*, not *to* saints. So, I will say again: We Catholics must be careful how we talk about saints. Our non-Catholic friends could well get the incorrect impression that saints themselves possess divine power, when of course, it is God alone who grants divine favors.

We *do* look to saints as our personal patrons or patrons of specific causes: calling on St. Anthony for help in finding those perennially lost glasses or keys; St. Jude for seemingly impossible situations; St. Lucy for eye trouble. Then there are our personal patron saints, the ones for whom we are named or with whom we feel a special affinity. One of my favorites is the twentieth-century English mystic Caryll Houselander, with her spiritual outreach to people with mental illness, who were generally forgotten by society.

Occupations also have their patron saints: St. Cecilia for musicians, St. Francis De Sales for writers, St. Michael for police officers, and, of course, St. Joseph is the patron of carpenters. Regarding the saints in this book, St. Joan of Arc is the patron saint of soldiers and St. Catherine of Siena of nurses. While St. Francis of Assisi is the patron for environmentalists, I would certainly place Hildegard of Bingen in that category also. And St. Damien is a fine patron for people who experience any type of alienation. Mother Teresa of Calcutta said that if she ever were to be canonized (we probably should say *when* she is canonized), she should be considered a saint of those who suffer from a dark night of the soul, as is demonstrated in the chapter about her here.

Since I began my writing projects about saints ten years ago, there has been a massive revival of interest in them. Scores of books have been published and a simple online search will yield thousands of returns, making it easy to find out about individual saints.

I frequently have been asked how I choose the saints I write about. First, I need to be able to identify with them: to connect with their spirit and like them as people. Also, I need sufficient information about the individual's life, preferably from their own writings. Some of the saints in this book have left us a treasury of their spiritual writing. For others, like St. Joan of Arc and Henriette Delille, there is adequate contemporary evidence about them. After spending months researching, reflecting upon, and writing about each individual, I feel honored to consider them my spiritual friends.

I would like to make a special note about the chapters on Hildegard of Bingen, St. Catherine of Siena, and St. Joan of Arc. Modern medical science is looking in the rearview mirror when it attempts to diagnose religious and historical figures centuries later. While their diagnoses may be correct, that does not negate the fact that God works through our struggles as well as our joys. If Hildegard actually did suffer from migraines, Catherine truly was anorexic, and Joan actually was epileptic, then God used their conditions as channels of grace.

These stories were never meant to be exhaustive biographies. Rather, I hope that readers will use them as springboards to get further acquainted with the individual saints to whom they feel drawn.

CHAPTER ONE

HILDEGARD OF BINGEN
(1098–1179)
Healing and Visions

Sybil of the Rhine, prophetic visionary, ecologist, Europe's first botanist, brilliant musical composer, theologian, first woman doctor—these are but some of the many appellations given to the incomparably talented Hildegard of Bingen over the centuries. Arguably the most famous woman of the twelfth century, Hildegard referred to herself simply and lyrically as a "feather on the breath of God." Were she alive today, undoubtedly she would be in the vanguard of trying to protect God's creation.

Hildegard of Bingen was born in 1098 to a noble family in Böckelheim, Germany. Her parents offered her, their tenth child, to God by placing her with their family friend, the highly regarded Jutta, who lived at the Benedictine monastery of Disibodenberg. It was not uncommon at that time for families to offer a child to the church as a gift, or oblation. St. Bede of England was sent to a monastery at seven years old. Hildegard's parents did not realize what a jewel they were giving away in their daughter, a jewel that lay buried for centuries in dusky obscurity, until it was uncovered to sparkle gloriously nine centuries later. Their daughter is as well-regarded today as she was in her own time.

As a child, Hildegard was not always well. Beginning a lifelong pattern, she had long periods of illness during which she could not walk. She also saw brilliantly vivid visions, which she kept to herself when she realized no one else had them. Jutta, her teacher and mentor, aware of her young charge's considerable intelligence, taught her how to chant the psalms and the Divine Office in Latin.

Anchoresses

At that time, all nuns and monks lived secluded, cloistered lives in order to avoid worldly distractions and focus completely on prayer. Some, known as anchorites or anchoresses, chose an even stricter approach and were completely sealed off from the outside world in *anchor holds*. Anchor holds were usually attached to a church and had windows through which food could be passed. Probably the most famous medieval anchoress is the English mystic Julian of Norwich, who was granted several visions of Christ while she was seriously ill. (I tell Julian's story in *Saints to Lean On: Spiritual Companions for Illness and Disability*.)

Disibodenberg was a monastery of monks; Jutta and Hildegard, as the only women, lived secluded in the small anchor hold attached to it. On All Saints Day, 1112, at the age of fourteen, Hildegard dedicated her life to God as an anchoress by professing the vows of chastity, poverty, obedience, and, unique to the Benedictines, stability. To emphasize her death to the world, the enclosure ceremony included psalms chanted from the Office for the Dead. As medieval women always required the protection of males, Jutta and Hildegard were under the authority of the monastery's abbot.

As anchoresses, Hildegard and Jutta lived a strict lifestyle. The Benedictine Rule included praying the full Liturgy of the Hours each day. This meant rising at two AM to chant Matins, the hour-and-a-half long first Office of the day, then Lauds at dawn, Prime at six AM, Terce at nine, Sext at noon, and None at three PM, Vespers in the early evening, and concluding with Compline right before retiring. Manual labor, studying, and food preparation took place between the hours of the Office. Food was eaten in moderation: only one meal in winter and two in summer.

Jutta had acquired a reputation for dispensing wise counsel and spiritual direction, and began to attract other young noblewomen, gradually turning the tiny anchor hold into a convent. After Jutta died in November 1136, Abbot Cuno appointed Hildegard superior of the fledgling convent.

By now in her early forties, Hildegard reveled in her new autonomy. While still answerable to Abbott Cuno, she now had the freedom to order her and her nuns' lives as she saw fit. Although far from the norm for cloistered women, and directly contradicting the Benedictine Rule, Hildegard permitted her sisters to grow long, flowing hair and to wear attractive dresses for Mass. Prior to her appointment, she had lived in silence and submission, with no avenues to express her inner life with its extraordinary visions. Now, Hildegard's pent-up creativity burst forth with a vengeance.

The Music of God

Hildegard of Bingen is considered one of the first known composers of polyphonic music. Part of an abbess's role was composing music to be chanted during liturgies on special feast days. Learning to chant new music over and again is not easy. It requires energy and a good memory, to say nothing of frequent practice. As Hildegard considered her music to be inspired by the divine in praise of the divine, she insisted that her nuns practice it to her satisfaction.

Fortunately, much of Hildegard's music has survived, probably carefully preserved by her Benedictine sisters down through the centuries. In all, she composed seventy-seven chants and a morality play set to music entitled, "The Ritual of the Virtues." Her chants are gathered into a work known as "The Symphony of the Harmony of the Heavenly Revelations," or simply *Symphonia*. Not surprisingly for this extremely gifted woman, her music, ancient as it is, is still performed and lauded for its originality today. A simple Internet search of "Hildegard music" yields thousands of references to Hildegard's sacred music.

Visions and Headaches

From an early age, Hildegard experienced visions, which she was careful not to reveal, for fear of what others might think. These visions were cosmic in nature, accompanied by brilliant color and light, and filled with beautiful imagery: fire, mountains, flowers, and trees. Hildegard always attributed her myriad accomplishments in music, theology, and natural medicine to her heavenly visions.

Hildegard made it clear that she was not hallucinating. In her most famous work about her visions, *Scivias* ("Knowing the Ways of God"), she insists that they came from God:

> But the visions I saw I did not perceive in dreams, or sleep, or delirium, or by the eyes of the body, or by the ears of the outer self, or in hidden places; but I received them while awake and seeing with a pure mind, and the eyes and ears of the inner self, in open places, as God willed it.[1]

When some people experience migraine headaches they describe "seeing" bright flashing lights. Similarly, Hildegard's descriptions of bright lights and accompanying visual effects have lead modern neurologists to suspect that her visions may have been caused by migraine headaches. Acclaimed British neurologist Oliver Sacks, after studying Hildegard's accounts of her visions with their accompanying illustrations, reached the same conclusion: "A careful consideration of these accounts and figures leaves no room for doubt concerning their nature; they were indisputably migrainous...."[2]

Migraine headaches are a neurological condition, often accompanied by nausea and vomiting; they are different from stress or tension headaches, as they can last up to three days, with pain often felt only on one side of the head. Migraine pain can be debilitating, often requiring bed rest. There is no cure at this time, but there are medications to ease symptoms. As with other hidden conditions, migraine sufferers are subject to a lack of understanding from others, as the severity of their pain is not clearly visible.

For Hildegard, far more important than their origin is what her visions were about. In *Scivias* she describes twenty-six visions in detail and accompanies them with doctrinal explanations. The book consists of three sections: the first part deals with creation, the second with redemption, and the third salvation, in which at times Hildegard is speaking for God and at other times for herself.

An important theme running through *Scivias* is *veriditas*, or "greenness." Hildegard used *greenness* to signify the freshness, vigor, and strength of the natural world. On a deeper theological level, *greenness* referred to the grace of the Holy Spirit animating all that exists: "And I will sow in that field roses and lilies and other perfumes of virtue, and I will water it constantly with the inspiration of the Holy Spirit...."[3] As this selection shows, Hildegard used the natural imagery of a field. Her deep love for God's creation is apparent all through *Scivias,* as it is filled with lovely metaphors linking nature to the spiritual: "For as wine flows out of the vine, so My Son went forth from My heart;..."[4] and "...the soul flows through the body like sap through a tree."[5]

Each section of *Scivias* begins with a detailed description of a vision, and then explains its meaning. In a beautiful example in Book Two, vision two, Hildegard vividly describes her vision of the Trinity:

> Then I saw a bright light, and in this light the figure of a man the color of a sapphire, which was all blazing with a gentle glowing fire. And that bright light bathed the whole of the glowing fire, and the glowing fire bathed the bright light; and the bright light and the glowing fire poured over the whole human figure, so that the three were one light in one power of potential.[6]

She explains the symbolism of the vision, stating that the bright light designates the Father, the sapphire-colored man symbolizes the Son, and the glowing fire represents the Holy Spirit. She then offers a sound doctrinal explanation of three-in-oneness:

> And this means that the Father, Who is Justice, is not without the Son or the Holy Spirit; and the Holy Spirit, Who Kindles the Hearts of the Faithful, is not without the Father or the Son; and the Son, Who is the plenitude of fruition, is not without the Father or the Holy Spirit.[7]

"Write the Vision Down"

In the book of Habakkuk, God instructs the prophet: "Write the vision; make it plain on tablets..." (Habakkuk 2:2). Although using parchment rather than tablets, Hildegard also received a command from God to write down her visions: "...I heard a voice from Heaven saying to me, 'Cry out therefore, and write thus!'"[8] Together, Hildegard and Volmar, the monk who was her longtime friend and secretary, spent hours in Disibodenberg's scriptorium, while Hildegard dictated and Volmar recorded her visions. Volmar, wanting to determine if these visions were divine or demonic in origin, reported Hildegard's visions to his superiors, who in turn notified the pope. As the church was ever vigilant about demonically inspired heresy, Pope Eugenius III dispatched a delegation of learned clerics to Disibodenberg to determine if Hildegard's visions were of God. After much questioning and perusing, their consensus was an emphatic yes—these messages indeed were from God.

Hildegard herself needed assurance about where her visions came from. She wrote to the Cistercian monk Bernard of Clairvaux, famous for his asceticism as well as his writings, asking for his help. Assuring him that she understood their meaning, she went on to relate the cost of not speaking about her visions for so many years: "In the meantime, because I have kept silent about this vision, I have been laid low, bedridden in my infirmities, and am unable to raise myself up."[9] From struggling with her lifelong debilitating illnesses, Hildegard was clearly aware of the physical cost of suppressing her visions. Bernard's reply was to view her visions as grace and be true to their messages.

Hildegard probably had another reason for writing to Bernard of Clairvaux. As a bit of a politician, she was seeking an endorsement, especially from a highly regarded man, since women were rarely taken seriously in the twelfth century. Hildegard was fortunate that two of the most powerful men of her time, Pope Eugenius and Bernard of Clairvaux, endorsed her visions and her theological thought. Had they not, Hildegard would today be no more than an interesting footnote to the century, a minor medieval mystic and herbalist.

The Synod

Synods are gatherings of church leaders to discuss matters of doctrine. At the 1147 Synod of Trier in Germany, Pope Eugenius, greatly impressed with Hildegard's visions, read parts of *Scivias* to the assembly. Bernard of Clairvaux, also familiar with Hildegard's work, also praised Hildegard's visions and the quality of her theology.

Until this point, Hildegard had a reputation among the local people as something of a sage, dispensing wise counsel to all who asked. Now, however, she became a celebrity, one of the most famous women in all of Europe, consulted by kings, bishops, and common folk and earning her reputation as the "Sybil of the Rhine."

Rupertsberg

Hildegard had lived at Disibodenberg for over forty years. However, with her growing fame, more and more young noblewomen (who brought with them their dowries of significant sums) wanted to enter her community. The increasing number of nuns made the tight quarters of the anchor hold even more cramped. Speaking in a vision, God told Hildegard to leave Disibodenberg and found a new monastery for her nuns at Rupertsberg, near the town of Bingen. She informed Abbot Cuno of God's command; he, however, refused permission for them to leave. Having the famous visionary Hildegard on site brought Disibodenberg a great deal of prestige.

Distraught at being denied permission, Hildegard became ill: "I could not see any light because of a clouding of my eyes, and I was so oppressed down by the way to my body that I could not raise myself. So I lay there, overwhelmed by intense pains."[10] She was virtually paralyzed, in extreme pain, and at times unable even to see. Her condition caused Abbot Cuno to relent, and Hildegard and her nuns left Disibodenberg for the barren rock on which sat the ruins of the former monastery of Rupertsberg.

Both literally and figuratively, this was an audacious move on Hildegard's part. Her new foundation would require rebuilding the monastery itself, as well as establishing a mill, garden, and barns. Always innovative, Hildegard contrived a system of pipes that provided running water. Life was difficult at first; food was scarce and the constant presence of the male laborers was a disruption to community life. Some of the nuns could not abide the primitive conditions and left. However, gradually, under Hildegard's supervision, the buildings were constructed and normal convent life resumed.

Herbs and Healing

Part of convent life involved restoring sick people—other nuns, monastery workmen, or visitors—back to health. There were two sources of medical care in the Middle Ages: doctors, sometimes called "surgeons," and women who specialized in healing. Hildegard, like many women of her day, knew a great deal about the healing powers of various herbs and plants; knowledge that had been passed down from generation to generation. Generally, women were not permitted to assist anyone outside of their own home. Because of her reputation as an accomplished healer, people from far and wide flocked to Hildegard to be made well. As in so many other areas, Hildegard the healer went beyond the usual strict boundaries for her sex.

Hildegard firmly believed in what we call today "holistic health," stressing the importance of the connections between body, mind, and spirit. She wrote, "The soul loves moderation in all things. Whenever the human body lacks measure, and eats and drinks or something like that unbalances it, the powers of the soul are wounded…. So in all things let people maintain a proper balance."[11]

Considered to be the first known woman doctor, some modern physicians have examined Hildegard's healing practices in light of contemporary medicine. Dr. Marcia Ramos-e-Silva, writing about her specialty of dermatology, notes that Hildegard was the first woman to write about the treatment of skin diseases: "Many of her remedies, even for internal diseases, operate through this organ [the skin], such as rubbings, baths, warming, sauna…."[12] Some of Hildegard's treatments remain in use, such as the soothing and healing properties of calendula, chamomile, and aloe. She recommended that butter should be eaten in moderation, and that salt was good, but not to excess. She also recommended spearmint to aid digestion.[13] On the other hand, her recipes involving boiled hamster and dead mice certainly do not appeal to our modern palate!

Wanting to make her medical knowledge available to others, Hildegard systematized and categorized plants and their healing effects, writing two scientific works: *Physica* and *Causae et curae*. *Physica,* which discusses the curative powers of various herbs and plants, is a cornerstone of botany and is thought to be one of the earliest books on natural history written in German and the foundation of botanic studies in northern Europe.[14] *Causae et curae* examined underlying causes for diseases as well as their various cures. Both books, in addition to providing a window into how medicine was practiced in the twelfth century, contain information still useful in the twenty-first.

Interdict

By the end of her life, and although growing frail, Hildegard remained a highly acclaimed celebrity. Her fame, however, did not protect her from struggles with the church she loved. Several months before her death, a conflict broke out between her and the local clergy. Hildegard, as was the custom, permitted a nobleman to be buried in the monastery grounds. This upset the clergy, who claimed that the man had been excommunicated and should not have been laid to rest in consecrated ground. When Hildegard refused to disinter the man, her monastery was placed under interdict, or ecclesiastical censure. The interdict prohibited the nuns from chanting the praises of the Divine Office or even hearing Mass. This was painful for the Hildegard, for whom chanting the liturgy was a divine mandate, a practice of praise she cherished.

Not one to remain passive when threatened, the eighty year-old abbess wrote to the clergy, informing them that God had revealed to her in a vision that a terrible fate would befall the monastery if the man's body were to be disinterred. They remained unmoved. Finally, Hildegard went over their heads, stating her case in a passionate letter to the archbishop himself. After rebuking her for her disobedience, he relented and lifted the interdict. Hildegard's chants echoed once more through the monastery of Rupertsberg.

Shortly after, on September 17, 1179, God called Hildegard of Bingen, abbess, healer, theologian, and so much more, home. She had succumbed at last to one of her debilitating illnesses. The woman who all her life had considered herself merely a "feather on the breath of God," floated gently home to chant forever among the choirs of angels.

Reflection

"Greenness"—what a lovely word! Leave it to Hildegard, one of the most creative minds that ever existed, to come up with a concept of freshness and vigor that remains utterly fresh and vigorous today. As a gardener and botanist, she had a deep reverence for the earth, and the interconnectedness of its natural systems: the rising and setting of the sun, the eternal sweep of changing seasons, and the dying and rising of the seeds that become life-sustaining food.

I firmly believe that our earth belongs to God. It is only on loan to us, to sustain and refresh us. Hildegard, speaking in God's voice, writes in *Scivias*: "But when I choose, it bears so abundantly that people have the fullest...."[15] Hildegard knew that the fruits of earth are pure gift from God and we have the job of being its stewards.

I am sure that Hildegard of Bingen would be appalled at the condition of God's creation today: melting glaciers, tops of mountains removed, and antibiotic-fed cows and chickens crowded into tiny pens that prevent them from moving. She would firmly support Pope Benedict in his many appeals asking people to protect God's creation.

While I was on a recent retreat, I began to reflect on this new science of quantum physics, about which I knew virtually nothing. I was especially struck by neutrinos, teeny particles smaller than an atom. Neutrinos flow from the sun to earth, then through our bodies, and out to the universe. This strikes me as a metaphor for how grace works, flowing from God through us and then out to others, connecting us to one another and to God's earth in that delicate balance that is the web of life—the same web of life that Hildegard of Bingen so revered.

CHAPTER TWO

St. Catherine of Siena
(1347–1380)
Healing the Church

Catherine of Siena's writings have earned her the distinction of Doctor of the Church, achieved by only two other women, Teresa of Avila and Thérèse of Lisieux. Possessed of an unusually strong will, Catherine was a problem to her parents as a teenager, and had what would today be considered an eating disorder. Yet she went on to become one of the most influential voices in the Catholic Church in the Middle Ages. She was a woman of great spirit and extraordinary spirituality.

Most saints live their entire lives in obscurity: Their holiness becomes known only after they die. Not so with St. Catherine of Siena, whose sanctity was as well known in her day as it is today. Her many letters give us great insight into her life, her spirituality, and her complex personality. Clearly, her soul was a window through which others could glimpse God.

Aside from her own letters, we have an extremely detailed biography of Catherine of Siena, written by her spiritual director and friend, Bl. Raymond of Capua. Raymond was a gentle and perceptive man, and at first he was less than enthusiastic about taking on Catherine, because he had questions about her.[1] He wisely anticipated criticism of his portrait of Catherine, and took care to list his sources at the end of every chapter. These consisted of his observations, eyewitness accounts from family members and friends, or Catherine herself.

Family

Catherine Benincasa (meaning "good house") was born the twenty-third of twenty-four children. Her father, Giacomo di Benincasa, was a dyer; her mother, Lapa, the daughter of a local poet. Giacomo was successful in his trade and was able to support his large family. Mother Lapa was strong-willed and resourceful, but not as strong-willed as her daughter, the future saint.

When Catherine was twelve, her family began to consider a good marriage for her. Their daughter, however, would have none of it. She resisted strenuously, for in her mind she was already consecrated to her Beloved. She did consent to her mother's wishes for a brief sojourn with her older, married sister, Bonaventura, who took Catherine under her wing and taught her how to become a marriageable young lady of Siena. Catherine adored her older sister and began to apply herself to learning the ladylike skills of hairstyling and makeup. But, in the midst of these lessons, Bonaventura died in childbirth.

Despite her deep grief at the loss of her sister, young Catherine's sanctity was deepening. Daily, she grew closer to God and extended charity toward others. The pressure on her to marry remained. Not being married was quite common among many female saints of the church: Clare of Assisi, Kateri Tekakwitha, Teresa of Avila—all resisted married life.

It can be a bit startling to realize that as great a saint as Catherine of Siena actually gave her parents the runaround while she was in her teenage years. Catherine's rebellion was typical for an adolescent; however, what she was rebelling *about* was not typical. Catherine was deeply in love with Jesus. Hence she would not hear of marriage and, interestingly, had no desire to enter a convent. To fend off increasing pressure to marry, she even cut her beautiful long hair—an act that infuriated her parents, for it made Catherine completely unmarriageable until her hair grew back.

Irate that Catherine had cut her hair, her parents retaliated and enforced a family edict that prohibited Catherine from withdrawing to any place by herself. She was given many arduous household tasks, so she neither had the time nor place to pray.[2]

Probably many teenagers would respond to this by pouting, throwing a tantrum, or rebelling against these strictures. Catherine of Siena's deep relationship with Jesus gave her the grace to live the Gospel invitation to turn the other cheek. She coped in two ways. First, she turned the punishment into a joy by imagining her father as Jesus, her mother as Mary, and the rest of the family as the disciples. Serving the Holy Family was a pleasure; no task too lowly or sordid to undertake for them.

Second, deprived of her small prayer room or cell, Catherine carved out her own cell in her heart, as Raymond of Capua noted: "The result was that she...now remained uninterruptedly within the walls of that inner cell of the heart which no one could take from her."[3] Who today has not felt the need for a place of solitude away from the "madding crowd," a place that is sacred and conducive to deep prayer? This great mystic has an answer: We can, as she did, retreat to our own "heart cell" and meet Jesus there.

Finally, emboldened by a vision of St. Dominic, Catherine con-
fronted her family: "Be advised by me, and put a stop once and for
all to any matchmaking in my regard. This is a matter in which I
have not the slightest intention of yielding to your will. I must obey
God rather than man."[4] Giacomo Benincasa issued a new edict
commanding his family to allow Catherine to pray as frequently as
she wished, with no further pressure to marry.

Sisters of Penance of St. Dominic

In the fourteenth century, women had two options: marriage or the
convent. Autonomy for women was unheard-of; women simply
did not live on their own. We have seen Catherine's strong resistance to marriage. Why, then, did she not choose a convent? I wonder if Catherine possessed an intuitive sense that, in addition to a
deep prayer life, she was also to minister with people who were
poor. Such activity was not possible for nuns then; all communities
were cloistered and never engaged in any ministry of direct service
to God's people.

Catherine of Siena had only the option of entering a cloistered
convent or a "third order;" where women lived under vows. In
Siena at the time there was a third order consisting mainly of widows: the Sisters of Penance of St. Dominic. Wearing a black mantle over a white dress, they were known as "The Mantellates."

Catherine aspired to join the Mantellates of Siena. She begged
her mother, Lapa, to ask the group to permit her to join them.
Halfheartedly, Lapa did so. At first the sisters replied that it was
against their practice to give a habit to young women; rather it was
given only to widows and those with "unblemished reputation."[5]
Perhaps the sisters were reluctant to have their own reputation hurt
by younger women who might eventually choose marriage. With

mixed emotions, Lapa informed her disappointed daughter of their decision.

Shortly after, Catherine became ill with some sort of pox; she had a high fever and lesions broke out all over her body. Seeing an opportunity, Catherine said plaintively to her mother: "If you want me, dear mother, to get well and strong, you must satisfy my longing for the habit of the Sisters of Penance of Saint Dominic. If not, I am very much afraid that God and Saint Dominic...will not leave me with you much longer...."[6] Even Catherine of Siena could be a bit manipulative!

Lapa, eager to save her daughter's life, managed to persuade the sisters to relent. They agreed to interview Catherine with the stipulation that she was not to be too physically beautiful. They then dispatched a few sisters to determine Catherine's attractiveness level. Raymond of Capua tactfully describes Catherine: "...even under normal circumstances, she had nothing out of the ordinary in the way of good looks."[7] Now, due to her pox-ridden body, her true appearance was barely discernible.

Catherine passed not only the physical unattractiveness test, but a much more crucial one. The sisters were struck to their core by Catherine's spiritual maturity and common sense; she was accepted at once. Her illness disappeared and she received the black-mantled, white Dominican habit.

Austerities

The medieval mind-set was quite different from ours today. For one thing, Catholicism, with its different feasts, veneration of saints, and clearly defined rules, was the center of life in the towns and villages. In stark contrast to the "having it all" of today's culture, doing penance for one's sins and sacrificing for God's sake was a way of life. The great medieval saints were extremely strict with themselves, denying the pleasures of the flesh for the sake of growing in the spirit. Catherine was renowned in her time for her extreme austerities. Even prior to becoming a Mantellata, Catherine practiced harsh penances, sleeping on a plank and wearing wool clothing and a hair shirt in Italy's hot summer climate.

Even as these deprivations weakened Catherine physically, they strengthened her spiritually. She expressed her love for God incessantly with anyone who would listen. In an endearingly humble aside, Raymond confesses to occasionally falling asleep during these spiritual waterfalls of words, only to be chided by Catherine: " 'What do you mean,' she would say, 'by letting slip the profit of your soul for sleep? I might as well be talking to the wall as to you about the things of God.'"[8] Not even her spiritual director could keep up with the spiritual dynamo that was Catherine of Siena.

Retreat From the World
After becoming a Third Order Dominican, Catherine, desiring to deepen her relationship with Jesus, resolved to live the rule of her order stringently, and also to live in silence and seclusion. She stayed within her own "cloister," the small bedroom in her family's home, never leaving it except to go to church. During this time, she conversed frequently with Jesus. She confided in confession to Raymond: "...my only master and teacher was the Spouse of my soul, our Lord Jesus Christ. Sometimes he taught me by an inner inspiration, sometimes by openly appearing and speaking to me...".[9]

It is an axiom of spirituality that the closer one grows to God, the more active the evil spirit becomes, trying every conceivable trick to keep the soul from turning to God. This was the case with Catherine. She was tormented by doubt about her austerities. Would they lead to a physical or nervous breakdown? Was she being proud and setting herself up as better than others?

Catherine knew how to deal with these temptations. She never argued with the evil spirits, but rather relied on Jesus to help her withstand their temptations. In a vision, Jesus spoke to her from the cross: "My daughter Catherine, look at what I have suffered for your sake. Do not take it hard, then, when you too must suffer something for my sake."[10] And, "...For what I take pleasure in is not sufferings in themselves, but the generosity that accepts them for love of me."[11]

Catherine of Siena needed the spiritual grounding she received during her years of formation with Jesus; it intensified her already deep relationship with Christ and fortified her for the struggles ahead. For Jesus now asked Catherine to observe the two greatest commandments: Love God, and love your neighbor as yourself. He assured her that her love for her neighbor would bind her even more tightly to him.

Confident that Jesus was with her, Catherine set out upon her new ministry of continual service to people in need. Her typical day consisted of rising early in the morning, anonymously delivering food or clothing to needy families, and then visiting sick people. Catherine had a special empathy for people who were ill, which is why she is the patron saint of nurses.

Accused

Life became difficult for Catherine after a serious allegation was circulated against her by one of her patients. Andrea, also a Sister of Penance of St. Dominic, had breast cancer. There was no treatment at the time and the cancerous sores emitted a foul stench. No one had the stomach to visit Andrea, let alone care for her. Into this void stepped Catherine. After a time Andrea began to resent Catherine and made stinging remarks to her. Far worse, though, was the fact that Andrea circulated rumors that Catherine was not living her vow of chastity.

The Sisters of the Mantellate were understandably upset by these rumors. After all, this was the very situation they had feared in accepting a younger woman such as Catherine. They resolved to determine whether there was any truth to the allegations.

They sent a few sisters to interview the sick woman. Andrea persisted, insisting that Catherine was engaging in unchaste behavior. The sisters also interviewed Catherine, repeating the accusations that Catherine was no longer a virgin. Catherine denied the allegations and "meekly and modestly" replied that she was indeed still a virgin.[12]

Catherine returned to nurse Andrea, with her customary devotion. Overwhelmed by Catherine's kindness, Andrea felt chastened. Sending for the Mantellate sisters, Andrea contritely recanted her story, adding that she believed that Catherine was truly a saint.

Just as the accusations against Catherine had spread quickly throughout Siena, the news of her vindication spread as quickly. As Catherine was already known for good works and deep piety, this act of love and forgiveness for a woman who had sinned against her revealed that Catherine was, indeed, a woman who walked closely with God. Her reputation for sanctity grew, accompanied by a growing reputation for something else.

Inedia or Anorexia

The phenomenon of eating little or nothing is not new; it is documented as far back as the Middle Ages, when it was called *inedia*. Today, we know this condition as anorexia nervosa, as serious a condition in Catherine's time as in our own.

Anorexia nervosa is defined as an aversion to food due to some personality disorder. Rudolph Bell explains in his book *Holy*

Anorexia how people with anorexia nervosa starve themselves to the point that their lives are at risk.[13] Today, millions of women, as well as men, cope with this eating disorder. People with anorexia are seeking a sense of identity; exerting their own will is of paramount importance. Anorexic individuals may listen dutifully to family, friends, counselors, and then do what they want, eat little or nothing. Threats, punishments, rewards—nothing entices them to eat.

While culturally worlds apart, the psychological need for control and autonomy underlie both the twenty-first and the fourteenth-century anorexic woman. Medieval women were likely rebelling against a patriarchal structure in society and church; modern women obsess about their culture's worship of being thin. Sadly, death is the ultimate outcome if the disease is not treated.

Whether fasting to be holy or fasting to be thin, people with anorexia are heavily influenced by their culture. Holiness was held in high regard in medieval times; thinness is virtually worshiped in today's society. An additional shared characteristic is the tendency toward perfectionism: the need to be perfectly holy, the need to be perfectly thin.

It is important to note that our attitude today toward our bodies is quite different. As we are made in the image and likeness of God, and our bodies are temples of the Holy Spirit, we are to treat our bodies with reverence and care. Extreme austerities are discouraged; rather, most spiritual directors invite us to pray with the inherent asceticism already provided by our physical and emotional wounds and pain.

Was Catherine Anorexic?

Was St. Catherine of Siena a "holy anorexic"? She certainly exhibited some basic characteristics: a strong will, along with a deep desire to be holy and in total union with Jesus. She also lived life on her terms, refusing marriage and the cloister, and instead becoming a Third Order Dominican and remaining with her family.

As Raymond indicates, even in her own day, people were skeptical of Catherine of Siena's austerities, especially her extreme fasting. Our world today is even more skeptical. We moderns demand proof. Many of us do not allow for divinity to enter the human realm.

As believers know, however, there are those inexplicable and unfathomable instances when God intimately touches our lives. Clearly, God's hand was on his beloved Catherine. The grace that permeated her soul flowed over into her physical being, strengthening her to live her asceticisms. As her biography states: "The familiar presence of the Lord to her was the grace from which came the prodigies which were a feature of her life..."[14]

Catherine as Healer

Catherine was a spiritual rock star of sorts in Italy. After the incident with Andrea, the people of Siena viewed her as heroic not only for forgiving Andrea, but also for continuing to care for her. In addition, Catherine performed many miracles; healing souls and minds as well as bodies. Catherine was able to convert even the most hardened of people, convincing them to reform their lives. People with epilepsy or severe mental illness were also healed through her intercession. Raymond himself recounts how Catherine's intense intercession (she refused to leave his bedside until he recovered) healed him from the plague.

As word spread about this woman with prodigious spiritual gifts, other cities began inviting her to visit. Reluctant at first, Catherine eventually agreed, traveling to cities in central Italy.

Becoming ever more famous, she began a voluminous correspondence with people from every walk of life, including the pope, who consulted her about her native country and its looming civil war and factions. Catherine of Siena became a diplomat as well as a mystic.

Corruption in the Church

The fourteenth century was one of the most corrupt in the history of the Catholic Church. Popes strove for political power and huge incomes; cardinals lived like princes; "pardoners" dispensed absolution for a fee; priests ignored their vows and lived sumptuously and unchastely.

Due to the fighting in the territories around Rome, the papacy moved to a safer location in Avignon, in southern France. There, life for the popes and the curia was much easier, safer, and certainly more luxurious. Their lavish lifestyle and spiritual neglect of the faithful drew much criticism.

Catherine's profound love of Christ and deep reverence for the church caused her to be horrified at these abuses. She set out to heal her beloved church. It was her firm belief that the papacy should return to Rome, its original home. With the inner, God-given conviction that motivated her in everything, she started writing to Pope Gregory XI, dispensing spiritual advice and advising him to return the papacy to Rome. Thus began her political career as an advocate for church reform.

It is fascinating to read about Catherine's relationship with Pope Gregory XI. He granted her an audience in 1376 and they corresponded frequently. Pope Gregory was a weak and vacillating man, easily influenced by those around him. Catherine's letters to him are a mixture of affection, advice, and, of course, profound spirituality. She felt free enough to call him "Bobbo," Italian for

"Daddy." She encouraged him in very strong language: "Do not be a timid boy, be a man! Open your mouth and take the bitter for the sweet!"[15]

Finally, Catherine's attempts to persuade Pope Gregory were successful. After Gregory set out to return to Rome, he encountered hostile forces and his advisers wanted him to return to Avignon. Almost persuaded, Gregory decided to speak to Catherine before making any decision. After a lengthy conversation, she convinced him to continue. The young woman from Siena had managed to prevail upon the timorous pope to begin healing the church by restoring the seat of Peter.

Final Days

On January 29, 1380, Catherine collapsed in a church in Rome. She was in and out of consciousness for the next several weeks; her years of austerities had finally caught up with her. Catherine suffered greatly as she lay dying. When conscious, she dictated her last will and testament—her spiritual advice to her followers and to us.

First and foremost, she advised, we must love God and detach from all other human loves. She also emphasized the importance of humble, faithful, and persevering prayer. Then she exhorted her followers to avoid the temptation of judging others: "For *no* reason whatsoever ought we to judge the actions of creatures or their motives."[16]

Advice on forgiveness was her next topic: She said that whenever she had suffered persecution, she never held a grievance against her attackers, instead attributing their motives to zeal for the salvation of her soul. Rather, she thanked God for the grace to not be judgmental. Her final spiritual recommendation was simple: "Love one another as I have loved you." Then Catherine of Siena concluded with a promise which would be echoed centuries later by Blessed

Kateri Tekakwitha and St. Thérèse the Little Flower: "I promise you that I will be with you altogether and be of more help to you in a life beyond than it has been given to me to help you in this world, for I shall have left darkness and passed into everlasting light."[17]

Love, forgiveness, prayer—the example St. Catherine of Siena gives us for our own journeys of healing so that we, too, will leave darkness and pass into everlasting light.

A Prayer of St. Catherine

Jesus, gentlest love, you have loved me indeed, and by this you teach me how much I ought to love myself and my sisters and brothers. Love is had only by loving. For you have loved us so much, even though you have no need of us as we have of you.[18]

Reflection

St. Catherine of Siena's impact on the Catholic Church has been enormous. Raymond of Capua's account of Catherine's life, along with her own voice speaking in her letters, are great gifts to us. Her writings encourage us to live as authentic Christians; her life shows us *how* to live as authentic Christians.

The incident with Andrea, the woman with cancer, demonstrates not only Catherine's ability to forgive, but also her pouring out of herself to others in need. Forgiving someone who has made every attempt to sully your reputation is magnanimous; continuing to care for the person is downright heroic.

What motivated Andrea to attack Catherine in such a personal way? Why would a desperately ill woman want to ruin the life of her sole caregiver? While we will never know, Andrea was likely dealing with anger: anger about her disease, anger about her pain, anger that she was no longer able to do what she used to do. Most likely angry with God, she directed her anger at Catherine. Her anger is understandable; what she did with it is not.

Those of us who live with a significant level of illness or disability can relate to Andrea's situation. Most of us go through a range of emotions in the early stages of coping: anger, depression, grieving, bargaining with God. This is normal, we would not be human if we did not experience some hard emotions about what is happening to us. This is the time to seek support, whether from a friend, spiritual director, or therapist.

When I was first diagnosed with rheumatoid arthritis at age twenty-five, I was not at all sure what to do with my emotions. My Irish Catholic background did not encourage sharing deep emotions. Occasionally, I tried sharing with others, but in an attempt to cheer me up, they would point out how much worse things could be. True, but not exactly consoling.

It took me a while to see the whole picture. I loved Jesus and knew he loved me in return. I began to realize that what was happening to me was important. Important to Jesus; important to me. Through prayer and spiritual direction, I started to turn over the physical suffering to him while at the same time inviting him to work ever more intimately in my heart.

This was a great grace in my life. St. Ignatius of Loyola's famous prayer "The Principle and Foundation" invites us to see human conditions (wealth or poverty, sickness or health), as opportunities to serve God. My invitation was to give the pain, fear of the future, grieving over physical losses, lack of understanding from others—everything about my disability—to Jesus, to turn it all over and ask that it be used in whatever small way to heal wounds in the Mystical Body of Christ.

CHAPTER THREE

ST. JOAN OF ARC
(1412–1431)
Healing France While Hearing Voices

Joan of Arc. *Saint* Joan of Arc. A young woman whose legend has come down through centuries, inspiring women of all ages to transcend barriers, determine their own lives, and listen to God. In this chapter, I try to imagine the heavenly voices as Joan may have heard them.

There have been voluminous books written about Joan of Arc. It is easy to see why—she was a young woman who fought with men in battle at a time when women never stirred from the domestic hearth. She insisted on wearing armor in the days when slacks for women did not even exist. Her public life was as short as her legend has been long—while she was only in the public arena for nine months of her life, her story has fascinated the world for over six centuries.

Joan of Arc is a canonized saint and more: She is a national hero of France, especially of the city of Orleans. Unlike Catherine of Siena and Hildegard of Bingen, Joan did not provide hands-on healing, indeed she rather enjoyed the excitement of battle. She did, however, heal her country. She did this by restoring French confidence and morale at a time when France was almost subsumed into England, to be France no more.

In order to understand the significance of Joan of Arc, it is necessary to know the history of France at the time. Joan was born during the Hundred Years' War between England and France. A dispute over who was the real king of France had been going on for decades. Henry V of England invaded France in 1415 and won an unlikely victory against a larger French army at the Battle of Agincourt. As France's King Charles VI was mentally ill, he was unaware of his wife Queen Isabella's underhanded scheme to give France to the English by marrying their daughter to their enemy Henry V.

Complicating matters for France was the fact that Philip, the Duke of Burgundy, sided with the English. He joined forces with Henry V, forming an alliance known as Anglo-Burgundians. The conflict dragged on for years with southern France remaining loyal to King Charles, while northern France sided with the English and Duke Philip. After decades of war on their soil, the French people were divided, depressed, and completely demoralized.

War and More War

Into this world of conflict was born a young peasant girl named Joan in January, 1412 in Domrémy, in the province of Lorraine. Her father, Jacques d'Arc, was a farmer and respected leader of the town. Her mother, Isabelle, taught her how to pray and how to perform domestic tasks. Joan lived the life of a typical French peasant girl.

Until the day her voices came.

Voices of God

> *Joan, Joan, do not be afraid. I am of God's voice. I love you deeply. I will help you save your soul. You must keep yourself pure always. One day I will send you to crown your king and save France.*

When she was thirteen years old, standing in a field next to her father's house, Joan distinctly heard a voice speaking to her. It was noon; the voices were accompanied by a shining light. This was the first of many occasions when Joan heard the heavenly voices.

From the time of her trial for heresy, there has been great skepticism about the authenticity, as well as the origin, of Joan's voices. During the trial her interrogator asked if the voices were not of her imagination. Certainly they were, Joan replied, how else would God speak to her if not through her own imagination?

This was the first example of vast speculation through the centuries about the origin of Joan's voices. Was she mentally ill? Psychotic? Schizophrenic? This question has intrigued medical scientists for centuries.[1] Certainly, diagnosing a condition of someone who died over six hundred years ago is, to say the least, problematic. However, the general consensus by the medical community has been that Joan of Arc was schizophrenic.

More recently, however, theories have swung toward the disease of epilepsy. Epilepsy is a neurological disease that causes abnormal activity in a person's brain. People with epilepsy are subject to seizures, or brain malfunctions. Seizures can be caused by hormone fluctuations, stress, lack of sleep, and sensitivity to light.

Millions of people have been diagnosed with epilepsy; some of these have a form that is difficult to control, even with medication. The disease can strike at any age, but tends to be diagnosed more frequently among children and older people. Fortunately, children sometimes outgrow epilepsy.

As both noise and light accompany a type of epilepsy known as "ecstatic," the fact that Joan's voices were usually accompanied by church bells and always included bright light indicate that she may indeed have had epilepsy. However, the mystery of Joan and her voices will continue for centuries and, as the authors Giuseppe d'Orsi and Paolo Tinuper of the article "I Heard Voices" contend: "...a compromise between the scientific and mystic, rejecting neither, will be the way to resolve the mystery of Joan of Arc."[2]

On a more profound level, though, would it matter if Joan did actually have epilepsy? God certainly uses any sort of physical or mental condition as a source of grace for the individual who experiences it as well as for others. The fact that Joan of Arc may have had seizures certainly does not mean that God cannot, and does not, use the exigencies of our lives to draw us closer.

Under intense questioning at her trial, Joan insisted repeatedly that her voices were divine. They taught her how to save her soul, sent her on a specific mission to crown her king, and correctly prophesied when she would be wounded in battle. While not a typical medieval mystic, Joan had a deep spirituality: She prayed often and intensely and knew her being was grounded in God. Her voices were integral to her being and her life.

Joan, it is time it is your time to be a warrior to save France, save your people, and crown your King go forth boldly enter into battle.

When she was nineteen, Joan's voices told her that her time had come to leave home and lead men into battle for France. Stealing away from Domrémy, she went to Vaucouleurs, home of Duke Robert de Baudricourt, a powerful knight loyal to Charles. On the way, she met Jean de Metz, a young knight who instantly became her ally. Through de Metz's influence, Joan was given an audience with Baudricourt. After hearing that her voices had told her that he was to help her crown Charles, Baudricourt initially thought her mad. Joan, however, with a gift for persuasion, convinced him to let her go to Charles's court at Chinon. Baudricourt provided Joan with a horse and allowed de Metz and several other knights to accompany her on the dangerous journey to Chinon.

La Pucelle

Out of the oak forests of Lorraine will come a virgin to save France, "ran the age-old prophecy of King Arthur's legendary wizard, Merlin."[3]

History is clear that, despite close proximity to the men who accompanied her into battle, sleeping next to them in fields and stables, Joan of Arc never lost her virginity. She valued her virginal state highly, referring to herself as "La Pucelle," or "The Maid." Joan was clearly signaling the purity and strength that the state of virginity conferred on a woman in the fifteenth century. Virginity at that time was revered as sacred.

Charles VII

The Hundred Years' War made the French people despondent. Their country was divided; morale was low. King Charles VI died in 1422, when Joan was about nine years old. His son Charles VII, known as the "dauphin," was not yet crowned.

The younger Charles was a timid, vacillating man, easily influenced by advisors. As Mary Gordon so aptly put it: "As a man, he wasn't worth a hair on Joan's cropped head; as a leader, he was weak, equivocal, and self-serving."[4] He wanted to be king, but was reluctant to enter into battle with the Anglo-Burgundians. Aware that Joan was on her way to his court at Chinon, Charles decided to test Joan by hiding himself among numerous courtiers to see if La Pucelle could identify her true king. Joan, however, recognizing the trick, quickly singled Charles out.

Battle of Orleans

Joan of Arc had a remarkable sense of the power of symbolism. The dauphin provided her with a beautiful banner. Blue and white, and embossed with fleurs-de-lis, it read "From the King of Heaven," a clear reminder of Joan's divine mandate. Charles also provided her with knightly armor. While the armor protected Joan in battle, wearing it caused her much trouble later.

Medieval cities were well-fortified and walled against attack. Opposing combatants had to resort to laying siege, not permitting food or supplies to enter. For seven months, the English army had been laying siege to the strategically and symbolically crucial city of Orleans; recapturing it would give the French a decided boost in morale.

Joan's presence was a catalyst for the French army: The courage of the young peasant woman leading them inspired the soldiers. Her presence and reckless courage on the battlefield provided the psychological healing her country so desperately needed: Joan's impact on the Battle of Orleans was vital to France's victory. Joan won the day by raising the spirits of the French and inspiring them to follow her in her courage and daring.

Count Dunois, known as "The Bastard of Orleans," was in charge of the city. He wanted Joan's army merely to bring in supplies, not actually liberate the city. As the reputation of La Pucelle preceded her, Dunois courteously rode out to welcome Joan. No doubt expecting a sweet young virgin, he instead encountered an irate woman dressed in armor, who informed him that the military advice from her voices was superior to his mere earthly wisdom. Joan placed such stock in her voices that she had no trouble dressing down a member of the French aristocracy!

Daughter of God, you will lead them into battle. Your shoulder will be struck. You will feel pain, but this wound will heal and will not hinder you long.

On May 7, 1429, Dunois ordered an attack on the English troops outside Orleans. At his side was Joan the Maid, astride a white horse with her beautiful blue-and-white standard flowing in the wind. Despite what she heard her voices warn her—that she would be wounded in her shoulder—Joan fearlessly charged into battle. Sure enough, during the fighting an arrow pierced her armor in her left shoulder, exactly where her voices had predicted. Although in great pain, Joan had her wounds tended and returned to battle. After several more hours of fighting, the French drove the English from the city of Orleans. At long last, the French had finally won a decisive battle against the English invaders. The French forces were ecstatic.

Joan the Maid was dubbed the "Maid of Orleans," a title she retains to this day. The churches of Orleans rang with grateful "Te Deums." The tide of the war had shifted because of the fierce rallying presence and rapid military success of the Maid of Orleans. As Mary Gordon concludes: "In a week, Joan had accomplished what well-trained and well-organized captains had not been able to...in six months."[5] And she goes on further to say that Joan's triumph at Orleans went far beyond a military one: "The French needed someone like Joan, someone to break through their paralysis. She broke through and handed them a victory."[6] The French army regained its will to fight again; scores of men signed up to fight the English.

Joan was revered by the French, reviled by the English. To the medieval mind extraordinary events were of supernatural origin: either from God or the devil. To the English, anyone suffering

Joan's wound and returning to battle must surely be a witch. They longed to have her in their hands.

Le Roi

The first part of her mission accomplished, Joan now wanted to finish it by crowning Charles VII. This required a lengthy journey to Reims, site of the magnificent cathedral where French kings were traditionally crowned. However, as the journey lay through unfriendly Burgundian territory, Charles, hardly a courageous man, hesitated at the danger. Finally Joan prevailed upon him, saying, "Now the time has come for you to begin to make preparations to go to Reims, where like the Kings of France, your predecessors, you will be anointed and crowned."[7] Finally persuaded, Charles was crowned King of France on July 17, 1429. In an unprecedented move, Joan the Maid, not only a commoner, but a *woman*, stood next to him during the coronation. After Charles was crowned, Joan, with her flair for the dramatic, sank to the ground weeping and embracing Charles' legs.

Her mission now accomplished, Joan could well have retired from battle and returned to Domrémy. But Joan chose a different path.

Captive

It is coming closer, chere daughter, freedom will end soon. Your enemies will take you. Do not fear. We will be there. We will help you.

Joan wanted to drive the English and Burgundians from their entrenched position in Paris. Charles, listening to advisers unfriendly to Joan, was reluctant. Joan prevailed and fought several skirmishes in small towns near Paris. Finally, trying to take the town of Compiegne, Joan of Arc was pulled from her horse and taken prisoner.

After being a knight in the chess game of war between France and England, Joan was now a pawn. She was initially held by Burgundians in the castle of Beaulieu, but after attempting to escape, Joan was moved to the more secure castle of Beaurevoir. Here she was treated humanely, even kindly, by the noble French ladies of the household. Meanwhile intense negotiating was going on for the right to try her. The English were desperate to get their hands on this woman who had humiliated them so often. Finally, for a huge sum of money, the Burgundians handed Joan over to the English, who placed her in their prison at Rouen. That was the end of humane treatment for Joan, whose plea to be held in a kinder church prison was denied.

Despite the fact that Joan had restored him to his throne, Charles VII did nothing to assist Joan in her gravest hour of need. He made no attempt to ransom or to free her. Her faithful companions who had fought next to her in battle also deserted her.

Heretic

The charges against Joan were numerous: heresy, witchcraft, idolatry, and "unseemly behavior"—for wearing men's clothing. Heresy was probably the most serious: Claiming one's directives came directly from God rather than through the mediation of the church was decidedly heretical. Inquisitions, tribunals called by the church precisely to root out heresies, were just beginning. Since the charges were ecclesiastical and the trial conducted by the church, Joan should have been held in a church prison, where nuns rather than English soldiers could attend her.

Joan's many months of imprisonment were barbarously cruel. She was chained to her bed; a narrow window permitted only a sliver of light. She was guarded by five Englishmen day and night. They tormented her and tried to rape her.[8] Joan felt that wearing men's clothing gave her a modicum of protection; little wonder that she refused to take it off.

Inquisitor

Bishop Pierre Cauchon hated Joan with a passion. An Anglo-Burgundian, he was anxious to make a name for himself by trying the famous Joan of Arc. He gathered sixty learned ecclesiastics and scholars to attend him at the trial, who spent weeks preparing the charges and the questions they would ask Joan. Cauchon, however, completely underestimated La Pucelle, who believed that, as she was being tried by her enemies, she was under no obligation to answer all their questions.

Daughter answer boldly.

From the beginning, Joan cooperated only minimally. She refused to swear the oath her accusers wanted: After being told to swear on the Gospels to tell the truth about everything she would be asked, Joan answered: "I do not know on what you may wish to question me. Perhaps you may ask such things as I will not answer."[9] Despite having no lawyer and facing harsh interrogations, Joan managed to confound the court with her straightforward answers on some occasions and refusal to answer on others.

Daughter of God, do not be intimidated but answer boldly. Believe what we tell you. It is our Lord's command.

Clearly the odds were overwhelmingly against Joan. Cauchon was determined to condemn her to death and questioned her for hours on end. When tired, he would ask another prosecutor to continue. Joan, completely alone, had to respond to these questions with no rest at all.

As the transcript of her trial has been preserved, we are able to hear Joan's voice and intelligence echo down through the centuries: "Are you in the grace of God?" Joan: "If I am not, then God put me there; if I am may He keep me there."[10] Asked about her virginity: "The first time she heard her voice, she vowed her virginity as long as it should be pleasing to God."[11] The voices were from which saints? "St. Margaret, St. Catherine and St. Michael."[12] Attempting to trip her up, they asked over and over again to describe the saints who spoke to her: What do they look like? Did they have bodies? Do they wear crowns? Are they always accompanied by light?

Another theme that ran through the trial was Joan's wearing men's clothing, her major transgression against societal mores as well as church law. Questioned again and again about why she wore men's clothes, Joan answered again and again that this was God's command.

> *Chere Jeanne, the time comes closer. Do not fear. We will walk with you beside you. Our Lord too will accompany you.*

Flames

After being imprisoned for over a year, her ordeal finally came to an end. Joan of Arc was declared a heretic and condemned to be burnt at the stake. On May 30, 1431, she was forced to put on a woman's dress and a dunce cap and was led weeping through jeering crowds on the streets of Rouen. According to Polly Schoyer Brooks's account, mounting the platform, "Joan fell to her knees and began to pray, asking to be forgiven as she forgave all who had condemned her, asking too that they pray for her. Many were moved to tears, even some of the churchmen who tormented her for so many weeks."[13]

As the fire was being prepared, Joan asked to see a crucifix; one was brought and placed in front of her to allow her to keep her eyes fixed on Jesus as she died.

The fire was lit somewhat away from her in order to prolong her suffering.

Oh my Jesus, I breathe no more black. All black my skin burns. All was for you…

When Joan was dead, the crowd demanded to see her unclothed, to be certain that she was indeed a woman. After displaying her dead naked body, officials cut it up and threw it into the Seine, ensuring that no relics would remain.

Rehabilitation

While King Charles and his court cared little about Joan's death, the people of France mourned for her. They loved their Maid for pouring out her life to restore the true monarchy of France. Years later, when Joan's prophecy that the French would finally drive the English from their land came true, King Charles VII started a rehabilitation investigation into her life and trial. Clearing Joan's reputation would further legitimize his kingship and end speculation that his crown was won through witchcraft.

In 1456, after a lengthy inquiry, including testimony from her eighty-year-old mother, Joan was cleared of all the charges against her. The proclamation of her innocence was read in the public square of Rouen, precisely at the spot where she had been burned.

Joan of Arc, La Pucelle, Maid of Orleans, became Saint Joan of Arc in 1920. It is claimed that after her body had been cut apart and thrown into the Seine, her heart was still beating. While this may or may not be true, the memory of their beloved Maid still beats strongly in the hearts of the people of France.

Joan of Arc's courage and passion make her a superb companion for us today. For people with any type of neurological condition like epilepsy or multiple sclerosis, Joan would certainly understand what their lives are like. While for a time hailed as a hero, Joan also experienced misunderstanding and derision because of her voices. This makes her someone to turn to for anyone diagnosed with mental illness, which unfortunately still has a stigma associated with it. Finally, there are times when all of us must reach down deep for the courage to do the right thing, even at great cost. This is when the Maid of Orleans, the young woman who defied the conventions of her time, invites us to turn to her to show us the way.

Reflection

It is impossible *not* to love Joan of Arc. Her passionate courage, her fierce independence at a time when women were merely property, and her answering boldly to the most learned ecclesiastics of her day—all are worthy of respect. There is another aspect of Joan, however, for which I have great admiration: She listened to the voice of God within. Even after being told countless times that listening to her voices was heresy, Joan was faithful to them until the end.

On a pilgrimage to Lourdes many years ago, I experienced God in a way I never had before. Of course, I wanted to be cured, to be rid of all this destruction in my body. However, shortly after being dipped in one of the healing baths, I knew immediately that it was not to be. Trying not to feel too disappointed, I got dressed and rolled my wheelchair over in front of the grotto where people were gathered for Mass.

Sitting in the middle of a sea of people also in wheelchairs, I tried to rally my flagging spirit. Then I felt a stirring inside of me...

a gentle nudge to look around. My long-held dream to minister with very poor people in developing countries or Appalachia was out of the question. But maybe my mission was right here in front of me. Perhaps the Spirit was inviting me to a deeper disability ministry, to use my God-given gifts to advocate for justice for this very marginalized group of people, of which I was a charter member.

I tend to dislike conflict; I have a "peace at any price" nature. I knew becoming a disability activist would be difficult; it would involve confronting systemic structures that were reluctant to change, structures that viewed my disabled friends and me as problems, not people.

I also knew that I would need the grace of courage, the courage that seemed to come so easily to Joan of Arc. Rather than riding a horse into battle, I would be riding in a wheelchair through the streets of Washington, D.C., fighting for justice and inclusion, the justice and inclusion that Jesus wanted for the disabled people of his time.

No, I was not physically cured at Lourdes, but through God's grace, I was definitely healed.

CHAPTER FOUR

VENERABLE HENRIETTE DELILLE
(1812–1862)
Healing the Slaves of New Orleans

I believe in God.
I hope in God.
I love.
I want to live and die for God.

This simple prayer was the credo of Henriette Delille, a free woman of African descent who deliberately chose to give up a life of privilege and prestige because of her profound love for Jesus. Amidst the insidious racism of her time Henriette Delille brought a healing touch to the lowest of the low, the slaves of nineteenth-century New Orleans.

We are all products of our environment and our ancestry. Where we were born, how we were brought up, and who our parents and grandparents were are crucial in determining the person we eventually become. For Henriette Delille, her ancestry not only defined her life, she embraced aspects of it that others in her family shunned.

Born in New Orleans in 1812, Henriette Delille was the daughter of a French father, Jean Baptiste Delille-Sarpy, and Marie Josef

Dias, a free woman of African descent. Marie Dias's mother, Henriette's grandmother, had also been a free African woman and her father, Antonio Diaz, a Spaniard. Thus, Henriette's family background included French, Spanish, and African ancestors. Today she would be considered multiracial.

There are few specifics about young Henriette's formal schooling. She most likely attended St. Claude School, begun by Sr. Marthe Frontier in 1823 and continued by the Ursuline Sisters in 1831. Henriette may have instructed other children in the school as she grew older. She obviously grasped the major tenets of Catholicism, however, she particularly understood the importance of the sacraments and Christ's command to minister to the least. Henriette was apparently deeply influenced by Sr. Marthe's life as a vowed religious and by her dedicated ministry to catechize slaves. By age fourteen, Henriette was completely absorbed in this work herself.

Plaçage

While life for free African American women in New Orleans in the nineteenth century was far better than it was for slave women, it was still a form of bondage. They were expected to participate in an unusual lifestyle that was clearly immoral but accepted: *plaçage*, the practice of a European man forming a sexual alliance with a young woman of color who was "refined, well-bred, and beautiful."[1] Generally, the white man was a wealthy aristocrat whose wife and family lived in France or Spain.

"Refined, well-bred, and beautiful" certainly applied to Henriette Delille. In addition to attending school, Henriette was being prepared by her mother to be a *plaçée*, and secure her future by forming an alliance with an aristocratic gentleman. She was fluent in French, had a refined taste in music and danced with grace.[2]

Despite her mother's thorough training in *plaçage*, there was a problem: Henriette wanted no part of being the mistress of a white gentleman. She stubbornly refused to attend balls and other social functions precisely *not* to meet a man of wealth. She knew her call was to a more spiritual lifestyle, one of love for God and service to God's people and she wanted to "lay down her life for God."[3] She was also aware of the immorality of a sexual union outside of marriage. Whatever her reasons, her decision not to enter into a sexual alliance was a shocking one for her caste and social standing.[4]

We can only wonder at the intense pressure that Henriette's family put her under, to accede to their desire that she become the mistress of a wealthy man. Henriette's struggle was similar to that of St. Catherine of Siena and of so many other women saints who resisted family pressure to marry. Henriette did not want to be a *plaçée*, she wanted to live the invitation of Jesus in Matthew 25:40: "Truly I tell you, just as you did it to one of the least of these who are members of my family, you did it to me."

It is clear that Henriette was a woman of profound spiritual depth who obviously felt called to follow the incarnate Jesus, the Jesus who himself chose to leave the security of a life as a carpenter in Nazareth in order to go among his people to heal and to evangelize. Almost eighteen hundred years later, Henriette did exactly the same thing, so that she could heal the bodies and souls of the slaves. Above all, she was an evangelizer. Slaves were not permitted by law even to receive an education, but Henriette was determined to at least teach them about God. Perhaps she knew from her own experience how much the awareness of God's love can assuage many human hurts. She also became an unofficial pastoral minister for Fr. Etienne Rousselon, vicar-general of the diocese, who often asked Henriette to serve as a godparent for baptized slaves.

Slavery

The sin of slavery in Louisiana had grown in proportion to the expansion of its sugar industry. In the early 1700s, the French transported and enslaved Africans to work on the sugar plantations that thrived in the rich soil around the Mississippi River. The slaves were kept in shackles and sold on the block to plantation owners. The slaves were under the complete control of the plantation owners, and were subject to barbaric treatment, particularly if they attempted to escape. No efforts to educate slave children were made; when no longer useful, slaves were often turned out on the street to fend for themselves. M. Shawn Copeland sums up the horrors of slavery: "Enslavement turns God's human creatures into objects of property to be bought and sold at whim, to be abused physically, psychologically and sexually."[5]

Companions

Just as goodness attracts goodness, good deeds attract good people. Henriette's deep spirituality and desire to serve destitute people drew like-minded women to her. Her closest friendship was with Juliette Gaudin, another free woman of color.[6] Initially the two formed a 'pious society,' meeting for prayer and religious discussion in one another's homes: "She organized a religious society for women of color...in the restricted area of social interaction for free people of color, a world adjacent to the world of slavery, where rights were minimal and legal protections precarious...."[7] Had she done nothing else, this alone would stand as a tribute to her spirituality and character. After a time, though, the pious society did not meet Henriette's need for a deeper expression of her spirituality. Along with Juliette and Josephine Charles, another friend in the society, Henriette longed for the structured life of a religious community.

"Free Woman of Color"
In New Orleans in the 1800s, as well as throughout the Old South, there was the "one drop" rule. No matter how white free people of color looked, they were considered black if even one percent of their ancestry was African. As may be seen in the only photo we have of her, Henriette Delille clearly looked white. In the census of 1830, however, she chose to register as a "free woman of color," even though other members of her family identified themselves as white. Deliberately choosing downward mobility was even more radical than refusing to participate in the *plaçage* system, as "passing for white was a common practice among free people of color since economic and social opportunities were so much better for them as Caucasians."[8]

The Catholic Church sometimes accommodates itself to the culture around it, in this case the evils accompanying slavery in the Old South.[9] Despite the church's tolerance of slavery, at the same time it did make efforts to baptize and instruct slaves. And despite it all, the young Henriette Delille knew she had a vocation to religious life.[10] She longed to live in a convent, sharing communal prayer and ministry with other women who chose to live for the love of God. She was thwarted, however, by her own humble claim of the status of a "free woman of color."

White Only
Determined to live out her religious vocation, Henriette applied to a religious community for admission. She was denied entrance however, for one reason: She was a woman of color. At that time, some orders in the church refused to accept black people (although this was not the universal policy of the church). Racism had seemingly killed her deepest dream.

One wonders how Henriette felt after having been told that she could not enter because she was part black. She must have known that religious communities could refuse anyone of African heritage. Had she hoped that her ministry to slave children would open doors? Did she have any regrets about having given up the status of a white woman?

We don't know the answers to these questions; we do know that Henriette Delille did not relinquish her dream of becoming a nun. If she could not be accepted into a white community, she resolved to start a black one. Accordingly, Henriette and her companions Juliette and Josephine decided to find a house where they could live together. They built a convent and hospice in New Orleans on St. Bernard Street to aid "aged persons, who are sick and poor."[11] Henriette was keenly aware however, that she needed to establish a proper convent for her small community, which was already attracting young women. On November 21, 1842, the group moved to a house on Bayou Road in the newly established St. Augustine parish, with Fr. Rousselon as their spiritual director. The Sisters of the Holy Family mark this date as their official founding, with Henriette, Juliettte, Josephine Charles, and Fr. Rousselon as their founders.

When Henriette's mother died in 1848, she left Henriette enough money to purchase land and to build a larger house on Bayou Road in New Orleans, naming the house after the Holy Family. There the three women taught students and lived a communal religious life. This life had many rewards and many hardships: Some evenings they had nothing to eat except sugar water, and their dress consisted only of a "Joseph's coat" of patchwork clothing donated by friends. Also, their ministry was not without danger. The laws in New Orleans regarding slaves were growing increasingly more stringent, restricting interaction among whites, free people of color, and slaves. The sentence for breaking these laws was hard labor for life or even death. Henriette and her sisters, as free women of color, were forbidden by law even to be with the slave children they were ministering to, let alone teach them.

Novitiate

In order to become a proper religious community, Henriette knew that she must undergo a novitiate, or period of formation. This would enable her to structure her own community along traditional lines, as well as to instruct any young women who wished to join her community. The problem was that no community for black sisters existed and the white communities did not welcome women of color. So Fr. Rousselon quietly arranged a period of formation with the Sisters of the Sacred Heart in an area outside of New Orleans. There are no records regarding this because all agreements were made orally due to the strict racial laws. Accordingly, in 1852 Henriette and Juliette lived for one year with the Sisters of the Sacred Heart, living the life of an established religious congregation, while learning how to instruct children in Catholicism.

By 1851, the Sisters of the Holy Family were formally established as a community under the protection of Bishop Antoine Blanc. Together they enjoyed many rewards while enduring many hardships. They gave every scrap of food and clothing they had to people in need. Life grew increasingly difficult during the 1850s as the Civil War approached. After the occupation of New Orleans by Union soldiers in April 1862, the city was in turmoil.

Healing Bodies, Healing Souls

Henriette Delille firmly believed in the health of the soul as well as of the body. Like Hildegard of Bingen, Henriette was skilled in the art of natural healing, using herbs and roots to cure people. Henriette's mother had taught her these healing arts, which had been useful in caring for sick slaves. However, Henriette was also aware of the power of the sacraments. Wanting to save souls as well as bodies, her primary mission was evangelization. The sisters instructed women of color and slave children in Catholicism; they also invited the elderly and dying people they cared for to turn to the faith and be baptized. Sometimes, dying people were simply taught to make the sign of the cross as an act of faith in their dying hours.

Death and Dispersion

There is no doubt that Henriette Delille lived the Gospel message deeply; she was on fire with love for Jesus and wanted to spread that love as far as possible. Her extreme work ethic and her bouts with illness, however, weakened her constitution. In the fall of 1862, Henriette was again ill. She died of tuberculosis at fifty years of age on November 17, 1862. Fittingly, she had a simple and inexpensive funeral and was buried in St. Louis Cemetery #2. Her obituary tells of the outpouring of love at her funeral Mass: "The large crowd that assisted at her funeral revealed by their grief the extent of the loss clearly felt for her who for the love of Jesus Christ had become the humble and devout servant of the slaves."[12]

Henriette was the glue that held together her small community of sisters.[13] This unity dissolved after her death, with seven of the twelve women leaving Bayou Road. Her close friend Juliette Gaudin became superior general, and eventually the small community of nuns again began to grow, carrying on the healing ministry of Henriette Delille. Small at first, the Holy Family Sisters grew steadily, eventually ministering in other parts of Louisiana.

Today, the Sisters of the Holy Family continue the mission of their founder. True to her vision, they continue to evangelize and to care for children, elderly persons and all who are disenfranchised. The community was devastated, however, by Hurricane Katrina in 2005.

Henriette, Sylvia, and Katrina

At 2 AM on August 29, 2005, Sr. Sylvia Thibodeaux, congregational leader of the Sisters of the Holy Family, had a strange feeling: "I had an eerie feeling, the air was very heavy. We knew that Hurricane Katrina was coming straight at New Orleans, moving quickly from a category three to a category four, and was now a category five."[14] Having experienced evacuation before, Sr. Sylvia knew the importance of having an evacuation plan: She signed a contract with an ambulance company to drive the elderly sisters from their motherhouse.

At nine in the morning on August 30, four ambulances arrived; they formed a convoy to head out of New Orleans. As they drove along, however, Sr. Sylvia noticed that the ambulances were not driving out of New Orleans, but rather downtown to the Superdome. Reacting quickly, she convinced the ambulance drivers to leave the city. The small convoy of ambulances carrying the sisters joined the mass exodus of people leaving their homes behind in New Orleans, some never to see those homes again.

Like so many others, the Sisters of the Holy Family sustained great losses during Katrina. Ten sisters died immediately; others later due to extreme stress. Their motherhouse in the Ninth Ward was completely destroyed; the sisters themselves were scattered around the country. Just as their early founders had pulled their community together again after Henriette's death, the Sisters of the Holy Family have returned to their ministries and reopened their nursing home and assisted-living facilities. Sr. Sylvia attributes this strength and resilience of her community to the spirit of Henriette Delille: "I believe Mother Delille was with us. This must have been like after her death...the sisters dispersed but returned and regrouped. We know our dear Mother Delille prayed for us."[15]

Community historian Sr. Mary Bernard Deggs wrote in the 1890's: "Would to God that many of our first sisters had lived some years longer to enjoy the fruit of their work, they who had toiled so hard in the beginning for the love of God."[16]

Henriette Delille lived out her wish of living and dying for God. For the love of God, she and her companions dedicated their lives to the least of the least in early New Orleans. The community they started, the Sisters of the Holy Family, continues to "toil hard for the love of God" among the neediest people in New Orleans today.

Reflection
What amazes me the most in Henriette DeLille's incredible story was her deliberate decision not to "pass." In nineteenth century New Orleans, her life would have been so much easier had she been perceived as white, rather than multiracial. That so many nonwhite people were eager to "pass," and use the opportunities that being white brought, says a great deal about the discrimination against African Americans prior to the Civil Rights Movement.

Having grown up in the 1960s in the suburbs of Philadelphia, I was totally oblivious of this desire of many African Americans to pass. However, later in my own life and my reluctantly acquired disability culture, I understood the need to pass. In the early years after my diagnosis, I wanted nothing to do with disability in any way. It was easier to pretend to others as well as to myself that I was perfectly "normal," that I could do what everybody else could.

After a few years, however, my attitude changed.

I was fortunate that my physical condition did not become significantly disabling for many years. I needed the time to come to terms with what was happening to me, to let the light of God's grace shine in this spiritual and emotional darkness. Also, I became aware of the disability civil rights movement, which insisted that people with disabilities are *people,* not, "burdens," or problems to be solved. We have gifts and capabilities in addition to our disabilities; we have all the personality quirks and traits that everyone else has. Most of all, it became clear to me that I could live a happy and productive life even with rheumatoid arthritis.

Over the years, I have come to view my life from a different perspective. Dealing with the challenges of being labeled, of being stared at, of people I barely knew insisting on asking "What's wrong with you?" of being accused of being "demanding" when I just asked to be treated like everyone else—all these struggles helped me grow stronger. Experiences like these help me realize that I can do more than just cope, that I am more than merely a survivor, that I can be proud to claim my identity in God as a woman religious with a disability.

CHAPTER FIVE

ST. DAMIEN OF MOLOKAI
(1840–1889)
Healing the Untouchables of Molokai

The island of Molokai lures visitors from first sight: Its palm fronds sway in the wind as sea-green waves lap gently at its shore. Molokai is one of the loveliest of the eight islands of Hawaii. But its beauty belies its history: For more than a century, anyone in Hawaii with the flesh-and-limb-eating disease of leprosy was forced into exile there. Removed from their homes and families, they were left to fend for themselves. Despite having significant disabilities from leprosy, they were expected to plant, plow, and till the soil for food to sustain them. With no shelter, medical care, or government services, life on Molokai was indeed a living hell.

Into this living hell strode an angel of mercy: a hard-working, humble priest named Joseph de Veuster, eventually to become world-renowned as Fr. Damien the Leper. This man was clearly sent by God to improve the wretched lives of the inhabitants of Molokai and to help these victims of the disease, outcasts of Hawaiian society, to realize they were priceless to God.

Where Hawaii and Belgium Meet

In the eighteenth century, England was dedicated to expanding its empire and discovering new lands. One of its most famous explorers was Captain James Cook, who discovered the group of islands we now know as Hawaii, naming them the "Sandwich Islands" after his patron, the Earl of Sandwich. Hawaii was officially "discovered" and Europeans, especially the English, began coming to settle and convert.

Sixty years after Cook's discovery of Hawaii, a peasant family in Belgium by the name of de Veuster welcomed Joseph, their seventh child, into the world. Poor in material goods, but rich in spiritual ones, the de Veusters were devout Catholics who had tilled the Belgian soil for centuries. Their son Joseph was strong-willed and not above playing an occasional prank. He also exhibited a serious spiritual side, and frequently went off by himself to wander the fields to pray. When time permitted, Mere de Veuster read to her children from *The Lives of the Saints,* which no doubt planted the seeds of young Joseph's future missionary call.

Pere de Veuster sent Joseph to an academy in Louvain to study to be a merchant. Auguste, Joseph's older brother, had already left home to enter the Congregation of the Sacred Hearts of Jesus and Mary, a missionary order of priests and brothers headquartered in Paris. Writing to Auguste, who had chosen the religious name Pamphile, Joseph confided his desire for religious life. Their father, after receiving pleading letters from Joseph and consulting his parish priest, reluctantly consented to the desire of his son's heart and permitted him to enter the Congregation of the Sacred Hearts as well. At age nineteen, sturdy and handsome, Joseph de Veuster embarked on his journey of religious life.

Sacred Hearts

The novice master was dismayed at his new novice's lack of education, especially in the classical languages of Greek and Latin, as Latin was the language of the church. Noting Joseph's strength and sturdiness, perhaps he could serve the congregation as a brother, the novice director thought, and accordingly assigned him to manual tasks around the monastery.

Pamphile, realizing Joseph could never become a priest without Latin, tutored him during their free time. What Joseph lacked in intellectual ability, he made up for in determination and eventually mastered the language of the Catholic Church. He now was permitted to study for the priesthood. In an example of what some might call "divine foreshadowing," Joseph chose the name "Damien." The first St. Damien and his brother St. Cosmas were physicians in early Rome who refused to accept payment for their healing services to the poor. Both were eventually martyred for their Christian faith. The parallels to Damien's eventual healing ministry are uncanny.

Missioned

Both Damien and his brother Pamphile longed to go to faraway lands as missionaries. After a request from the bishop of Hawaii, both brothers volunteered. Damien knew that, as he was not yet ordained, his chances of being chosen were slim. Still, he hoped and prayed. Four priests and three brothers were selected. Pamphile was one of them; Damien was not. Although bitterly disappointed, Damien tried to hide his feelings while he helped his brother pack.

At that time, however, a typhus epidemic broke out in Paris. Because he was ordained, Pamphile spent day and night ministering to the sick and dying. Finally his own body broke down and he contracted typhus himself. Damien nursed his brother, praying for his recovery.

After it became clear that Pamphile would not be well enough to make the arduous sea journey, Damien had an inspiration: If not his brother, why not himself?

Damien bypassed the usual procedure of requesting permission from his novice director first and impulsively wrote directly to his superior general suggesting he be sent in his brother's stead. Incredibly, the permission was granted and a jubilant Damien began to pack.

In early November 1863, after walking twelve miles to bid his mother and siblings a tearful farewell, Damien and the rest of the Sacred Heart contingent set sail. The journey took a full five months, sailing around Cape Horn and then north to the Hawaiian Islands, arriving on March 19, 1864, the feast of St. Joseph, for whom Damien had been named at birth.

Early Years

Bishop Louis Maigret was in dire need of priests, but was less enthusiastic about non-ordained brothers. He arranged for Damien to complete his studies for the priesthood at the Sacred Hearts College at Oahu; Bishop Maigret ordained Damien eight weeks later. Now prepared for his lifelong dream of bringing Christ to others through the sacraments, Damien's first assignment was on the island of Hawaii itself.

Kamiano

Fr. Damien flourished doing the Lord's work, to which he was so clearly called. He traveled his district, saying Mass and performing his other priestly duties. He learned the native language fairly easily. His parishioners, very fond of him and realizing his deep love for them, called him "Kamiano," their rendering of "Damien." Damien, young and vigorous, rode on horseback to his far-flung parishes. His priestly duties were not enough for his endless energy; he also used his carpentry skills to build several churches. His life, however, was soon to take a dramatic turn.

Leprosy

Just as the indigenous peoples of North America experienced the arrival of Europeans as a mixed blessing, so, too, did the native people of Hawaii. Along with improved government and administrative structures, the Europeans also brought disease.

For the Hawaiian people, the greatest scourge the Europeans brought was leprosy. Believed to have originated around the Nile River, leprosy, now commonly known as Hansen's disease, has afflicted humanity from at least 300 BC. It is identified by sharp nerve pain and itching at first. But, ultimately leprosy is a chronic and fatal infection that degenerates the tissues of the body, organs, and nervous system, and can lead to open sores and rotting flesh.[1]

The horrid treatment meted out to people with leprosy throughout the ages is notorious. We know from the Bible that lepers were ostracized from the time of Abraham through Jesus' day. In medieval Europe, lepers were either cast out into the forest and fields, or placed in hospitals, or "Lazar Houses." Conditions in these leper hospitals were appalling: Hundreds were crowded into small structures and medical care was virtually nonexistent.

Because of its long incubation period and the stigma that remains attached to it, leprosy can be difficult to diagnose in its early stages. It was a medical mystery until 1873, when a Norwegian scientist named G.H. Hansen discovered the bacteria that caused it. Genuinely effective drug treatments did not come along until the 1970s, however. And because of Hansen's discoveries, leprosy is curable today.

In Damien's time, however, in order to stop leprosy from spreading, the Hawaiian government issued a decree commanding all people with the disease to be exiled to the island of Molokai, selected primarily because of its remoteness. The geography of Molokai was ideal for isolating a community of people—steep rocky promontories effectively walled them off into one area. The government expected the exiled lepers, most with severe disabilities, to plant, till, and produce food for themselves. This was virtually impossible, as many of them had lost the use of arms and legs, due to rotting away of the flesh.

A Call Within a Call

Often, priests and religious are given a "call within a call," a unique ministry within their vocation for which they are especially equipped. For the rest of Damien's life, he would live his call within a call, ministering to the lepers of Molokai as their priest.

In May of 1863, Bishop Maigret invited his priests to concelebrate at the dedication of a new church on the island of Maui. Before Damien left his parish, he had a premonition that he would never return there. In *Damien the Leper*, the book that made Damien famous, author John Farrow quotes Damien: "I heard, as it were, an interior voice telling me that I should never again see my beloved neophytes nor my beautiful chapels...."[2] In a conference with his priests, the bishop spoke about his concern for the leprous people of Molokai, and asked for volunteers to serve there (a difficult request as he knew he was condemning whoever volunteered to an eventual death). Damien later wrote to his brother Pamphile: "...Mgr. Maigret, our Vicar-Apostolic, declared that he could not impose this sacrifice on any of us. So, remembering that on the day of my profession I had already put myself under a funeral pall, I offered myself to his Lordship to meet, if he thought it well, this second death."[3]

The same graced impulse that inspired him years earlier to flout his order's mission rules was in his heart now. He volunteered. With a heavy heart, his bishop agreed. A ship was leaving that very evening for Molokai; Damien was on it.

Molokai

Damien had heard of the wretched conditions in the leper colony, but the situation was far worse than he had anticipated. He wrote, "[the lepers]...abandoned themselves to their fate with apathy alternating with orgies. The stronger stole from the weak. The agonies of the dying were made more acute with the cruelties of starvation and exposure. A species of native beer...was easy to brew from the roots of a wild plant. Drunkenness became rife, rioting broke out."[4] Molokai was a dog-eat-dog community with the strong taking advantage of the weak. As there was no hope of getting better or getting off Molokai, despair and immorality predominated—why live by the mores of a society that had abandoned you to a slow and painful death?

Lacking a rectory, Damien spent his first few weeks sleeping under a tree. Although he was used to a sparse, ascetical lifestyle, surely sleeping under the stars, with no protection from insects, tree rats and other creatures of the night, must have been difficult, even for someone as fearless as Damien.

Damien's new parishioners were graphically described by John Farrow:

> They were without faces or if they had faces they were distorted beyond resemblance to any human shape. Where eyes had been there were craters of pus; and there were gaping cavities, disease-infected holes, that merged with rotting mouths, where noses should be. Ears were

pendulous masses many times their natural size, or were shriveled to almost nothing. Hands were without fingers and some arms were merely stumps.[5]

Damien was human: He had to struggle to never express the revulsion he felt at the physical appearance of his new parishioners. In particular, the foul odors coming from pus-filled wounds and squalid living quarters were particularly offensive: "I have had great difficulty in getting accustomed to such an atmosphere. One day, at a Sunday Mass, I found myself so stifled that I thought I must leave the altar to breathe a little of the outer air, but I restrained myself, thinking of our Lord when he commanded them to open the grave of Lazarus...."[6] After a time, however, he grew accustomed to the continual stench.

Fr. Damien intuitively knew that in order to win the hearts and minds of his new parishioners, he must not only refrain from revulsion, he must embrace their lifestyle. Well aware of the risk, he shared the native dish of *poi* with them, eating from the same bowls and drinking from the same cups. He would even pass around his pipe after a meal.

The "homes" his parishioners lived in were nothing but tree branches tied together with rope. The cemetery was in a deplorable state: only shallow graves had been dug, and the bodies tossed in with no coffins. As there was usually at least one death a day on Molokai, this was a serious situation. At night, wild dogs and hogs fed off the remains. Obviously, this would greatly offend anyone's reverence for the body after death; for Damien, it simply was unacceptable.

Damien was a man of action. Seeing a problem, he immediately tried to correct it. He set about gathering wood and making coffins; he constructed approximately two thousand in his years on the island. And thanks to him, his parishioners would receive the last rites and a proper burial.

More people on Molokai died from lack of medical attention than from leprosy itself. Damien, in the spirit of his patron, St. Damien, became a doctor as well. Because there was no resident physician, he administered drugs from his own supply and treated the sick.[7] After reading a medical book, Damien became a surgeon of sorts, excising infected limbs and dead bones. His operating room was a simple table. He lacked even protective gloves, let alone anesthesia. While performing these surgeries he realized that the infection and wounds were due to the filthy conditions in the people's homes. It was then that Damien recognized he needed to bring clean water into the colony.

Water

Water is one of God's most precious gifts to us, without it; no one survives more than three days. Today, conflicts over water rights take place among developing nations. Many families throughout the world are kept in poverty by the simple fact that the women must spend most of their day hauling water for drinking and cooking.

That was the case on Molokai. The lepers were forced to walk to a faraway ditch for their water; those who were unable to walk had to beg or go thirsty. There was no water for cleaning. Realizing that clean water was essential both for drinking and cleaning, Damien scouted the surrounding mountains and discovered a reservoir of clear water. After much letter-writing and badgering of the health authorities, materials were delivered to Molokai, and Damien and his assistants constructed a crude but effective water system.

Health Authorities

People who are capable of condemning their fellow humans to permanent exile without enough food or supplies clearly lack compassion. The fact that the health authorities were members of his own race, the race that had brought the disease to Hawaii, stung Damien and exacerbated the resentment of the people. Not a passive man, he began a lengthy and sometimes heated correspondence with the health officials, continually requesting more food and supplies. They were always slow in coming.

Eventually this angry correspondence with the health officials escalated. Damien was viewed as a troublemaker. The president of the board of health clearly considered people with leprosy subhuman, problems to be exiled and forgotten. To Damien, it was immoral to deny the basic necessities of life to people who were slated to die from a gruesome disease. Thus, the lines were drawn: Damien continually demanding more supplies and the board of health complying only minimally.

Damien's two primary faults were his stubbornness and his temper. He responded angrily when the needs of his people were not being met. Joseph Dutton, who joined Damien on Molokai several years later, writes: "(Damien was) vehement and excitable in regard to matters that did not seem to him right...and he sometimes said and did things which he afterward regretted..."[8] However, without his perseverance in requesting supplies, his people would have suffered even more than they did.

Morality

As already noted, there was a great deal of drunken, lawless behavior among the lepers when Damien arrived. He wrote:

When new lepers came, the old ones were eager to impress them with the principle: aole kanawai ma keia wahi—"In

62

this place there is no law." I was obliged to fight against such defiance of Divine as well as human laws. The consequence of this impious principle was that the people—mostly unmarried—were living promiscuously without distinction of sex, and many an unfortunate woman had had to become a prostitute in order to win friends who might care for her and her children.[9]

From Despair to Hope

Although he realized that this behavior stemmed from hopelessness and despair, the highly principled Damien would not tolerate it. To counteract this widespread despair, Damien instilled hope into the lives of his people by offering them meaningful work and many spiritual opportunities. Damien engaged anyone with any strength to assist in building huts; many women started to tend others by washing and bandaging wounds.

Obviously, Damien's primary ministry was spiritual—to offer the sacraments and daily Mass to the Catholics and the increasing number of converts on Molokai. Recognizing that the priest's deep love for them included risking his own death from their disease, the people of the colony were naturally drawn to what motivated this man—his passionate commitment to his God. More and more people asked to be baptized Catholic. And Damien's familiarity with the Hawaiian culture helped him to incorporate the native music and bright colors his people loved into liturgies, attracting even more to the faith.

Fame

Damien's humility kept him from seeking any publicity for himself. In his eyes, he was doing nothing extraordinary in choosing life and death among the people of Molokai. However, he always rejoiced when the plight of his people was published, for invariably donations of food, clothing, and money followed. The board of health cared little about Damien's people, but Hawaiian citizens cared a great deal.

From the beginning of his arrival on the island, Damien's self-sacrificing ministry was noted approvingly by the local Hawaiian press. One newspaper even called him a Christian hero. But these occasional reports about Damien and his people were infrequent; for the most part he ministered in relative obscurity.

Shortly before his death however, Damien became world famous after his brother published one of his letters. Damien, angry, wrote to his brother, Pamphile: "Once for all let me tell you that I do not like that done. I want to be unknown to the world and now I find, in consequence of the few letters I have written, that I am being talked about on all sides, even in America."[10] While difficult for him, the article had a quite beneficial result for his people. Gifts and donations poured into Molokai from all over the world. One gentleman even donated enough money to build an orphanage for the young girls of the colony.

Damien had been requesting religious sisters to help with nursing and education of children for many years. In 1883, his dream came true. The bishop of Honolulu sent seven Franciscan sisters (including Mother Marianne Kopp, now a candidate for canonization) to Molokai to minister alongside Damien. Doctors also began to visit the colony, offering much-needed medical care.

"We Lepers"

On a Sunday in June of 1885, Damien approached the pulpit to deliver his weekly homily. He had given no indication that anything was amiss until he began to address the congregation. Instead of his usual "My brethren," he calmly used two other words: "We lepers." This was his way of informing his people that he now stood with them in every way possible, to the point of sharing their fatal disease.

For several years Damien had suspected that leprosy was in his system, mostly latent and showing very few symptoms. One morn ing, however, while shaving, he accidentally upset a basin of hot water on his foot. Although the water burned his skin, he felt no pain at all. Losing complete sensation in a limb is one of the first indications of leprosy. Perhaps not surprisingly, Damien seemed almost to rejoice in his diagnosis, writing to his bishop: "I have no doubt whatever of the nature of my illness, but I am resigned and very happy in the midst of my people... I daily repeat from my heart, 'Thy Will be done.'"[11] He had shared life with the people of Molokai for twelve years; now he would share their death.

Shocked and saddened, the bishop demanded that Damien come to Honolulu for a new treatment for leprosy. Reluctantly, Damien complied. When he arrived at the hospital in Honolulu, the sisters there wept at seeing how debilitated he had become. As the treatment required long hours soaking in a hot bath, the lengthy inactivity became a torment to Damien. After a lifetime of continual activity, he simply could not idle away his hours in a bathtub. He was permitted to return to Molokai.

Last Days

Fr. Damien should have died within six months or a year from his diagnosis. The needs of Molokai however, kept him going for far longer. He continued his routine of bathing wounds and building cottages in addition to his sacramental ministry. In his forty-ninth year however, it was clear that death was approaching. He felt relief and peace knowing that his work would continue with Joseph Dutton and other volunteers.

Appropriately, he gave orders that he would like to be buried under the same tree which had sheltered him on his first nights on the island. In his last days his people came often to visit, crowding around as their beloved priest reminisced about his early days in Molokai and his life back in Belgium. He assured his people that he would intercede for all who were stricken with leprosy. On Palm Sunday, 1889, he died peacefully in his sleep. The disfiguring lesions from the leprosy on his face completely disappeared.

The news of his death circled the world, leading to much acclamation and honor in editorials. Although he was now dead, Damien's ministry was not over: Governments from India to England finally realized the plight of many of their own citizens with leprosy and began to improve conditions.

St. Damien the Healer

Damien de Veuster was canonized by Pope Benedict XVI on October 19, 2009. His feast day is May 10. While he will probably always be known as "St. Damien the Leper," perhaps a better name for him might be "St. Damien the Healer."

Although no longer the scourge of humanity it once was, Hansen's disease is still with us. With early diagnosis and antibiotics, leprosy is treatable. In the past few decades, however, another dread disease has surfaced: AIDS. Fortunately, people with AIDS are no longer treated like outcasts as the lepers of old. Medical science has made strides toward prevention and treatment. Were he alive today, Damien would surely be urging complete acceptance of individuals diagnosed with AIDS and advocating for funds for care, treatment, and research. Anyone living with AIDS or any other serious disease will certainly find an understanding companion and advocate among the communion of saints—St. Damien the Healer.

Reflection

Although he could not directly heal the leprosy itself, St. Damien did a great deal to alleviate other physical sufferings of his people: hunger, exposure, lack of medical care. Clearly he also provided spiritual healing and comfort through the sacraments. However, Damien also healed in a deeper way. He got inside his parishioners' experience by literally living their lives. Imagine someone loving you enough that he or she will risk death by choosing to live your life right by your side every day. This must have had a profound healing effect on the people of Molokai: A healing effect that sank down to the core of their soul and spirit.

Becoming one with others to this extent is living the Christian calling to the ultimate. As St. Paul writes in his Letter to the Philippians: "Let the same mind be in you that was in Christ Jesus, / who, though he was in the form of God, / did not regard equality with God / as something to be exploited, / but emptied himself, / taking the form of a slave, / being born in human likeness" (2:5–7). In the ultimate act of mutuality, Jesus *chose* to become human, to be with us and show us the way to God. All Christians are called to imitate Jesus' self-emptying love by loving and living mutually with each other. Not many do it with the fervor and total self-abandonment of Damien de Veuster, who wrote: "As for me, I make myself a leper, to gain all to Jesus Christ."[12]

St. Damien's example invites us to see who the "untouchables" in our own lives are. Do we try to understand the experience of someone who is seriously disabled or addicted or who has AIDS or mental illness? Of course, only a few of us may be able to live the lives of others as Damien did, to get inside their experience by living side by side with them and sharing the same food. But we can open our hearts to those who are different from us—whether physically, religiously, or ethnically. We can answer the call of Jesus to be his ambassador to those in our society who are "the least." We can turn to Damien the Healer—share with him from our hearts, ask him to intercede for us for a deeper understanding for those we find hard to know or love. His example and guidance can inspire us to new openness to those people who are different from us.

Let us open our hearts to others, just as he did before us—St. Damien the Healer—the magnificent martyr of Molokai!

CHAPTER SIX

ST. EDITH STEIN
(1891–1942)
AND
ST. MAXIMILIAN KOLBE
(1894–1941)
Healing During the Agony of Auschwitz

She was a convert; he was a cradle Catholic. She was a brilliant philosopher; he, a brilliant mathematician. He delighted his mother by becoming a Franciscan friar; she broke her mother's heart by becoming a Carmelite nun. They died within one year of one another in the most infamous of the concentration camps: Auschwitz. The virtue of human empathy echoed through both of their lives: She wrote about it; he lived it. Pope John Paul II designated them both not only saints of the twentieth century, but also martyrs.

Although they were almost exact contemporaries, St. Edith Stein and St. Maximilian Kolbe never knew one another. Yet they are linked in our religious imagination not only because of their deaths in the worst genocide humanity has ever seen, but because of their lives of profound self-emptying love for others.

Edith

Shortly after Kaiser Wilhelm became Emperor of Germany in 1888, Edith Stein was born in Breslau, Germany on October 12, 1891, on Yom Kippur, the Jewish Day of Atonement. She was the youngest child of a large Jewish family. Her father, Siegfried, died when she was only two, leaving his wife, Auguste, to manage the family timber business as well as her household of seven children. Young Edith possessed a remarkable memory for her age: her eldest brother delighted in teaching her the names of German classical authors and showing her off at parties. Beloved by all in her family, her mother, Frau Stein, was especially attached to her precocious youngest child.

Edith was gifted with extraordinary intelligence, earning many academic honors and distinctions. At university, she studied philosophy, becoming the disciple of German philosopher Edmund Husserl, and earned her doctorate in 1915. Husserl's specialty was phenomenology, which drew philosophical conclusions through the close observation of external phenomena. In 1916, after Husserl's assistant, Adolf Reinach, was drafted to fight in World War I, Edith took his place as the famous philosopher's assistant.

Maximilian

The future Fr. Maximilian Kolbe was born Raymond Kolbe into a devoutly Catholic Polish family. Raymond was welcomed into the world by Maria and Jules on January 8, 1894. Although a strict disciplinarian, Maria Kolbe found it difficult to control Raymond, who was full of mischief and pranks. One day, exasperated, she exclaimed, "My poor child, what will become of you?"[1] Her words profoundly affected her son, who posed the same question to Our Lady of Czestochowa, patroness of Poland. In an apparition, Mary showed him two crowns, one white, one red, and asked him to choose one. He chose both crowns, decidedly prophecies of his life and death to come. Young Raymond was deeply moved, and became obedient to his mother from then on. This was the beginning of his lifelong devotion to Mary.

Raymond's life was altered through the kindness of the town pharmacist, Mr. Kotowski, who taught him Latin and the other subjects necessary to pass the examination to attend school. Raymond proved to be a brilliant student, excelling in mathematics. In 1907, with his older brother Francis, Raymond entered a Franciscan Minor Seminary, taking the name "Maximilian."

Recognizing his intelligence, Maximilian's superiors sent him to study at the Gregorian University in Rome, where he made solemn profession in November 1914, immediately after the First World War broke out. Brokenhearted by the war among Christian countries, Maximilian decided to wage counter warfare. This warfare would be played out on a spiritual battlefield. Turning to his beloved Blessed Virgin, Maximilian formed the Militia of the Immaculata, or "M.I." He and other seminarians would be Mary's recruited "knights" to combat the evil forces with deep prayer and devotion to Mary.

Edith's Conversion

Generally, conversions take place in stages. Despite her devout Jewish upbringing, Edith Stein considered herself not merely a philosopher but also an atheist. In order to draw her close, God slowly planted seeds in the soil of her soul. The first of these was the influence of another philosopher, Max Scheler, the first Catholic she knew. A more profound effect on Edith occurred when her friend Adolf Reinach was killed in battle in 1917. Edith went to comfort his grieving young widow, astonished to find that the woman was accepting her husband's death with great peace and equanimity. Anna Reinach was Christian (later becoming a Catholic), and after an initial period of deep mourning, she had the grace to accept her husband's death. Edith was stunned by her calm acceptance and impressed by the effect that Christianity had on her friend.

The last, and most decisive, seed to bloom in Edith's soul was planted by St. Teresa of Avila. While visiting friends, Edith chanced upon a copy of Teresa of Avila's *Vida* (*Life*). Entranced, she read the book straight through, not going to sleep until the wee hours of the morning. Upon finishing it she concluded, "This is the Truth," writes Hilda Graef in her biography of Edith, *The Scholar and the Cross*. Shortly after, she purchased a missal and catechism, and began studying Catholicism.[2]

Edith Stein was baptized into the Catholic Church on January 1, 1922. She broke her mother's heart when she knelt before her to say, "Mother, I am a Catholic."[3] Edith was uncertain of her mother's reaction. Would her mother react with fury? Perhaps be so distraught as to disown her? After Edith's announcement, her mother was inconsolable and the two women wept together. Frau Stein could not comprehend why her daughter became a Catholic. Edith later wrote, "…one of the greatest sorrows in life…to be interiorly separated from those one loves."[4]

Maximilian and Mary

Maximilian, also a fervent follower of the One who said, "I am the Way, the Truth, and the Life," returned to Kraków in Poland in 1919, having earned doctorates in both theology and philosophy. He returned with a serious case of tuberculosis. As he was so unwell, he was assigned to the less strenuous task of being a professor.

Fr. Maximilian had a deep capacity to empathize with the struggles of others; his own experience with illness undoubtedly added to this. While visiting ill friars in the infirmary, he would assure them that God always uses the trials in our lives to bring good to others. He urged the nurses to empathize with the sick men, to put themselves in their places and try to understand what it is like to be ill. He was calm about his own illness, realizing the spiritual value in it: "All these trials...are very useful, necessary, and even indispensable, like the crucible where gold is purified."[5] This calm acceptance of his tuberculosis foreshadowed his calm acceptance of the tortures to come in Auschwitz.

In January of 1922, as Adolf Hitler was organizing the National Socialist Workers Party, Fr. Maximilian Kolbe published the first edition of *The Knight of the Immaculata*, a magazine devoted to the Blessed Virgin Mary written expressly for laypeople. Along with its focus on Marian devotion, *The Knight* also taught Catholic doctrine and catechism. Publishing *The Knight* became Maximilian's primary focus; its circulation grew quickly and it soon required a much larger space for its printing presses. Accordingly, Fr. Maximilian moved his publishing enterprise to the remote Franciscan monastery of Grodno, Poland.

Edith's Vocation
Never one to do things halfway, Edith Stein wanted to follow her inspiration—Teresa of Avila—and become a Carmelite. As her spiritual directors felt that Edith's philosophical work was crucially important, they discouraged her, arranging for her to teach at a Benedictine boarding school for girls in the town of Speyer. Teresa of Avila's *Vida* describes a search for union with God through contemplative prayer; Edith Stein's desire was to do the same. At Speyer, in addition to her teaching and philosophical writing, she

embarked on an intense prayer life. Edith was always in chapel long before and long after both the students and the Benedictine sisters. Although not yet a nun, she lived like one, adopting an austere lifestyle and simple dress.

For ten years, Edith Stein taught at Speyer. Meanwhile, in addition to doing her own philosophical work, she studied the intellectual roots of Catholic philosophy, especially St. Thomas Aquinas.

At the suggestion of her spiritual director, during the late 1920's Edith began lecturing about Thomas Aquinas and also about the status of women in German society. At a time when Hitler was restricting the rights of Jewish women, Dr. Stein focused on the need for women to be educated. Skewering the old-fashioned, romantic notion of women as nothing more than a man's adoring helpmate, she wondered aloud who was this "...grotesque, petty, middle-class, half-witted, caricature of the Old Testament view [of the strong woman]?"[6] Her reputation as a Catholic lecturer with a feminist focus grew, culminating in an address she gave to a Catholic audience in 1930, "The Ethos of Women's Vocations." It became obvious that it was time for her to leave Speyer in order to share her knowledge on a broader stage.

In 1932, Edith started lecturing at the University of Münster. As the noose of Nazism was tightening around Jewish people, however, she was forced to resign in 1933. Meanwhile, her sister Rosa also began contemplating converting to Catholicism, refraining from doing so as she was still living with their mother and did not want to inflict on her the pain of "losing" another daughter.

By this time, Edith longed for the cloistered lifestyle of her spiritual mentor. She was also keenly aware of the power of redemptive suffering. In a letter to a student she wrote, "This is a fundamental idea of all religious life, above all of the life of Carmel through voluntary and joyful suffering to intercede for sinners and to cooperate in the redemption of mankind."[7] The name she chose in Carmel, Sr. Teresa Benedicta of the Cross ("Teresa Blessed by the Cross") had deep meaning for her. Being blessed by the cross goes beyond accepting the cross to welcoming it as a means of connection with all suffering in the mystical body of Christ.

One night in September of 1933, Edith broke the news of her entrance into Carmel to her mother, evoking another tragic scene tinged with tenderness and love. Frau Stein, already made distraught by the vicious anti-Semitism occurring in Germany, barely moved as she heard the news. Her daughter, the renowned lecturer Edith Stein, was giving all up to retire from the world to be a Catholic nun. From now on she would see her beloved daughter very infrequently—only on visiting days and at ceremonies of profession. Sobbing, she retired to her room and slept little that night.

Edith Stein entered the Carmel at Cologne, Germany on the feast of St. Teresa of Avila, October 15, 1933.

Max's City

It has long been observed that when countries are experiencing difficulties, vocations to religious life often increase. As the Polish economy was suffering at the time, men and women entered religious life in increasingly large numbers. Soon men from the working class began to enter the Franciscan brotherhood, drawn to Fr. Maximilian's warm personality and his life work. A dilemma arose when more and more men wanted to become brothers, but only if they could work with Maximilian. They were accepted by the Franciscans, eventually growing to seven hundred brothers in all. In those times in religious congregations, there was an unfortunate separation between priests and the brothers. As the brothers were assigned to do the more menial household tasks, they tended to be looked down upon by the priests. Maximilian would have none of this. Instead, he advocated for the removal of class distinction, wanting all his men to be equal in the eyes of God.

After a time, the large numbers of brothers outgrew their monastery. It was clear that another larger location must be found. In what was certainly divine intervention, Fr. Maximilian miraculously received a grant of land near Warsaw. The building of Niepokalanow, the city of the Immaculata, began and flourished. Some years, two thousand men applied to become Franciscans at Niepokalanow, but only one hundred would be chosen, as Fr. Maximilian had high standards. Their ministry of publishing *The Knight of the Immaculata* grew steadily throughout the 1930's, with a circulation of one million by 1939.

Carmel

Sr. Benedicta was well prepared in some ways for the austerities of the Carmelite cloister, after living very simply, professing a private vow of poverty, and praying contemplatively. The famed Dr. Edith Stein was now a "little postulant," performing the mundane but necessary tasks of running a cloistered convent. For the first time in her life Sr. Benedicta was not good at what she was doing. Never having had to perform domestic duties, she was humbled by her slowness at learning the arts of sewing, washing dishes, and making beds. After a fault has been pointed out, Carmelite nuns are required to prostrate themselves on the floor, certainly another humbling experience. Sr. Benedicta embraced these crosses lovingly, offering them for the salvation of others.

Despite these trials, Sr. Benedicta was happy, describing living as a Carmelite as "profound peace." She wrote to her mother once a week, rarely receiving a reply. She was permitted to keep up contact with the outside world and also to continue her intellectual work.

Edith and Empathy

While Maximilian Kolbe was blessed with the gift of empathy, Edith Stein was not, at least early in her life. In "The Gift of Empathy," Normandie Gaitley, s.s.j., describes Edith's view of the philosophical concept of empathy as "the ability to participate fully in the experiences of others, as if with their eyes and feelings. We practice empathy when we put ourselves in the place of the other...."[8] After her entrance into Carmel, Edith reflected on the fact that she herself lacked this gift when she was younger: "I had always regarded it as my right to point out everything that appeared to me to be negative, to expose all weaknesses, mistakes and faults in others without sparing them and sometimes doing this with irony."[9]

Later, candidly admitting that she regretted this former tendency to revel in her intellectual superiority, she wrote: "...I had completely changed my attitude toward others and to myself. I was no longer interested in being in the right and always getting the better of others...."[10] Her profound prayer life with Jesus had helped to bring her to live out fully what had previously been merely an intellectual concept for her.

Maximilian in Japan

Fr. Maximilian's ministry was not limited to Poland. Through a chance meeting on a train with Japanese students, he asked and received permission to travel to Japan to establish a Franciscan monastery there. He arrived in the spring of 1930 and resided there for six years, publishing the Japanese version *of The Knight* and converting many to Catholicism. Also, despite skepticism and scant resources from his community, he built the second City of Mary, named "Garden of the Immaculate" near Nagasaki.

He was highly criticized on all sides because of his choice of location for his new Niepokalanow. Critics claimed that it was on the wrong side of the mountain, it faced away from the city, it was underneath a long ridge, and simply would not be a productive place. They were wrong. Fr. Maximilian had been uncannily prescient. Not only did the Japanese version of Niepokalanow flourish, the mountain and ridge protected it from the atomic bomb dropped on Nagasaki in 1945. Fr. Maximilian Kolbe's new City of Mary suffered only the minimal damage of windowpanes being blown out.

Always a workaholic, Fr. Maximilian had worked himself into a state of poor health. He returned to Poland in 1936 and was elected guardian (superior) of Niepokalanow, his very own foundation. At this time, the infection of Nazism was seeping throughout Europe. Rather than shunning these nationalistic, antireligious movements gathering steam around the world, Fr. Maximilian believed in studying them in order to counter their arguments. Forward-thinking as usual, he started a radio station to counteract Nazi propaganda in Poland.

Sr. Benedicta's Writings
Her Carmelite superiors were wise to allow Sr. Benedicta to continue writing. During her years at the Carmel at Cologne, Benedicta wrote both spiritual and philosophical works. Her great philosophical treatise, *Finite and Eternal Being,* later considered important for the renewal of Catholic philosophy, synthesized not only the phenomenological concepts of Edmund Husserl, but also the thinking of Plato, Thomas Aquinas, and Augustine.

Benedicta's mother died on September 14, 1936, the feast of the Exaltation of the Holy Cross, and also the day that Carmelites renew their vows. She relented toward the end and occasionally replied to her daughter's letters. Sr. Benedicta's sole consolation for her profound loss was that at least her mother would not have to witness the continuing horror occurring in Germany.

In addition to her intellectual work, Sr. Benedicta also wrote works of a profoundly mystical nature. Always proud of her Jewish heritage, her reflection "The Prayer of the Church," points out that Jesus, as a Jew, used traditional Jewish blessings at the Last Supper. These words have come down to us in the consecration of the bread and wine in the Mass. Her last mystical work was *The Science of the Cross,* an analysis of St. John of the Cross's *Dark Night of the Soul.* The cross and the suffering it symbolized were about to become a tragic reality for Benedicta.

Benedicta's New Reality

As Adolf Hitler's power and strength grew in Germany and throughout Europe, his Aryan agenda did as well. Jewish people in Germany were no longer permitted to be lawyers, doctors, soldiers; they were not allowed to own pets, and were only to sit on special yellow park benches. All, including Benedicta, had to wear the yellow star of David, which read "Jude," meaning "Jew." Then came Kristallnacht, the "Night of Broken Glass," on November 9, 1938. In retaliation for the murder of a German diplomat by a Jewish man, Nazi storm troopers set synagogues all over Germany on fire, looted Jewish stores, ransacked homes, and killed over ninety Jews.

It was clear that for her safety, as well as the safety of the other nuns, Sr. Benedicta had to leave the Carmel in Cologne. On December 31, 1938, a friend drove her to the Carmelite convent in Echt, Holland, where she was warmly welcomed. Eventually her sister Rosa joined her, living in an uncloistered section of the convent. Back in Germany, the Nazis closed all religious schools, putting priests and nuns out on the street.

Despite being cloistered, Sr. Benedicta and the other Carmelites in Echt were well aware of the increasing oppression of the Jewish people. Benedicta wrote: "The more an era is engulfed in the night of sin and estrangement from God the more it needs souls united to God.... The greatest figures of prophecy and sanctity step forth out of the darkest night."[11] Benedicta was horrified by what was occurring to her people. Her years of prayer before the cross helped her to remain calm even in the midst of great suffering, as she was so conscious of its profound value for the mystical body of Christ. She was also aware of the power of "souls united to God," individuals whose prayer and goodness bring light even to the deepest of darknesses.

Maximilian Requiescat

In February 1941, Fr. Maximilian, certainly a "soul united to God," and four other Franciscan priests were arrested and taken to Auschwitz. The men lived in "blocks" which were large rooms with bunk beds piled on top of one another; generally two men shared one of these beds, which consisted only of boards. Nights were always cold; summer days could be blisteringly hot and humid. Whatever the weather conditions, the men worked all day, building extensions of the camp.

Priests were among the lowest of the low, referred to as "priest swine." One day, the commander of Maximilian's block, known as "Krott the Bloody," forced Maximilian to carry a load that was far too heavy for his small frame. When Maximilian stumbled, Krott had him whipped with fifty lashes, leaving the priest more dead than alive.

Somehow, Fr. Maximilian Kolbe, whose health had always been frail, survived from day to day. He not only survived, but performed his priestly ministry as much as possible: hearing confessions, administering last rites, and offering consolation and spiritual advice. Performing each act of his ministry risked death. For Maximilian, who had long been a man of courage, his ultimate act of bravery was coming.

Toward the end of July 1941, a prisoner escaped from Fr. Maximilian's Block 14. For every prisoner who escaped, Commandant Fritsch chose ten others from that block to die from the slow torture of starvation and thirst. On July 28, Fritsch ordered the men to stand at attention in the blistering heat all day. Several died from heat exhaustion. Terror was in every man's heart. "We were lined up in drill order, and no one dared to move or attract attention to himself.... I stood directly behind Fr. Maximilian, so close I could have put my hand on his shoulder," said Mr. Ted Wojtkowski, one of the few survivors.[12]

Fritsch chose the ten men who would die. As Fritsch chose his final victim, Franciszek Gajowniczek, the man begged to have his life spared, calling out that he had a family. When Fr. Maximilian heard this, he stepped forward to address the commandant, in itself an act of bravery: "I wish to die for this man with a family." Nonplussed at this boldness, Fritsch asked him "Why?" Maximilian replied, "I am old and good for nothing,"[13] appealing to the Nazi practice of eliminating anyone who was physically weak. Fritsch acquiesced, and Maximilian joined the line of men marching to Block 13, the starvation block.

The men were pushed into a small, windowless cell with no sanitary facilities whatsoever. They were denied food and water. Death from thirst usually occurs within two to three days: the tongue and internal organs shrivel, and delusions and hallucinations can occur.

Maximilian Kolbe, although a victim, remained a priest. He consoled his fellow prisoners, hearing confessions and encouraging them to sing hymns together. The prison guards, stupefied with amazement, had never heard the dying men of Block 13 sing hymns before. Hearing the dying men singing, the rest of the prisoners in the camp joined in.

Amazingly, Fr. Maximilian did not die within three days, as most of the other men had. This man who had been frail his entire life, who lived with tuberculosis from his teenage years on, who had been whipped almost to death in the camp, refused to die in the manner and time frame to which he was condemned. After two weeks with neither food nor water, he remained alive. Exasperated, the Nazis injected him with carbolic acid on August 14, 1941. Fr. Maximilian Kolbe finally breathed his last. His body was cremated the next day, the Feast of the Assumption of his beloved Immaculata.

Franciszek Gajowniczek survived his years in Auschwitz and returned to his wife after the war.

Benedicta Requiescat

In July of 1942, the Dutch Catholic Bishops publicly denounced the Nazi treatment of Jewish people. Furious, the Nazis retaliated immediately, condemning the Catholic bishops for interfering, and announcing that all Jews and Catholic non-Aryans in Holland would be deported. On the evening of August 2, as the sisters were preparing for Vespers, two men from the SS demanded to see Sr. Benedicta. She protested that she was not to leave the enclosure, but they insisted that she come with them. Outside, her sister Rosa waited on the sidewalk. Edith, immediately knowing what was happening, took Rosa's hand and quietly said to her: "Come, let us go for our people."[14] Edith Stein was prepared. She had long identified with the strong Jewish women of the Bible: Judith, Ruth, and Mary of Nazareth, but particularly Queen Esther, who offered her life to save her people: "I am a little Esther, poor and powerless, but the King who has chosen me is infinitely great and merciful. And that is a profound consolation."[15]

Before being taken to Auschwitz, Sr. Benedicta and Rosa were in a transit camp at Westerbork. It was a tragic and chaotic scene with mothers so deeply in shock and despair they were not capable of caring for their children. A survivor of Westerbork remembered Benedicta's calm demeanor in the midst of this horror:

> [She] was just like an angel, going around amongst the women comforting them, helping them and calming them...[she] took care of the little children, washed them and combed them, looked after their feeding and their other needs.... She followed one act of charity with another until everyone wondered at her goodness.[16]

However, within a week of being taken from the Echt Carmel, Sr. Benedicta and her sister Rosa were dead. While no firsthand accounts of their actual deaths exist, it is safe to assume that, along with many other Jewish women and children who arrived at Auschwitz, they were all gassed shortly after their arrival. Edith Stein, Sr. Benedicta of the Cross, who had long embraced suffering for its redemptive value, now was able to offer the ultimate sacrifice of her life as her final sacrifice. Edith Stein now shared the fate of the Jewish people she loved in the crematorium of Auschwitz.

How can one ethnic group go to such extremes to destroy another? The Jews were Germany's scapegoats: All of the responsibility for the German sufferings in the early nineteen hundreds was incorrectly placed on their shoulders. They were blamed for Germany's defeat in World War I, and blamed for the rampant inflation and dire economic situation that followed.

Hate can be as strong as love. Through his Nazi party, Hitler stoked the fire of hatred against the Jewish people of Germany. As Dorothy Day wrote in 1933, "...Hitler owes his success to the fact that it is easier to arouse the people against something concrete like a race than against an idea."[17] Hitler bonded the German people in hate. What irony that this hatred produced two saints for the Catholic Church.

Martyrs as Well as Saints

Being canonized a saint in the Catholic Church simply means that the person's name has been inscribed in the canon, or list, of saints. The status of canonization does not indicate that the person has been *made* a saint, rather it is the recognition of that individual's holiness throughout life.

Pope John Paul II, throughout his long pontificate, canonized over six hundred saints—more than any other pope in history. Among the first he canonized, on October 10, 1982, was his countryman Fr. Maximilian Kolbe. St. Edith Stein's canonization took several decades, as many of the necessary records had been destroyed in the war. However, on October 11, 1998, Pope John Paul II canonized St. Teresa Benedicta of the Cross, citing her life of continual self-sacrifice for others, which culminated in her compassionate outreach for the women and children of the gas chambers of Auschwitz.

Were Edith Stein and Maximilian Kolbe martyrs? The word *martyr* means "witness." In the early days of Christianity, Christians who had been murdered because they would not deny Jesus Christ were called "martyrs." However, the term *martyr* also applied to: "...heroically virtuous persons who professed or exemplified their faith regardless of the consequences."[18] Both Maximilian Kolbe and Edith Stein certainly fit into this category.

Although they were contemporaries who never met, St. Teresa Benedicta and St. Maximilian Kolbe shared the ability to embrace suffering and offer it for others. They are fine spiritual companions to turn to in times of suffering and crisis. From the death camp of Auschwitz, Edith Stein and Maximilian Kolbe show us that suffering is not meaningless; rather, it can heal and soothe the wounds of the Body of Christ.

Reflection

When I was serving as Disability Awareness Coordinator for the archdiocese of Philadelphia, my team and I frequently presented an awareness program entitled "Welcome to My World." This consisted of nondisabled people donning darkened glasses, using wheelchairs, and performing different exercises to simulate deafness and other disabilities. The intention was that this experience would help participants to be more empathetic toward those of us who live with disabilities every day.

As empathy is difficult to measure, how effective this awareness effort was I will never know. Empathy is not pity; rather, it demonstrates respect. Empathy models being with; pity models looking down. I have never met anyone, disabled or not, who enjoys being pitied.

Both Maximilian Kolbe and Edith Stein realized the importance of empathizing with, rather than pitying, others. Sr. Benedicta realized later in life how hurtful her superior attitude must have been to others. Fr. Kolbe, on the other hand, urged others to be empathetic, to put themselves in the place of people who were unwell.

Empathy comes more naturally after we have been there ourselves. A friend of mine shared with me his impatience with his elderly mother about her slowness in getting out of a car. After his own back surgery, however, he knew what it was like for her,

"Then I understood how it is when your brain is telling your muscles to move and they're not able to do that. I thought of my mother right away, that this is how it was for her." He's now exceedingly more patient not just with his mother, but with all people who are able only to move slowly.

Empathy is an emotional application of the Golden Rule: We all need to support others as we would like to be supported. But this support must flow from a mutual respect. It is natural to feel a tug at the heart about some situations. (With all my years of disability ministry, I still feel my own tug at the heart at seeing children using their little wheelchairs or walkers). But it's important to move beyond that and relate to the person as a person, not a disease.

Our society is changing its attitude toward disability. As people with disabilities enter more into the mainstream of American life, they will be viewed as being people first, people who just happen to have a physical condition. When this happens, the Golden Rule of empathy will become the Golden Rule of life.

CHAPTER SEVEN

DOROTHY DAY
(1897–1980)
Healing God's Working Poor

She was tall, attractive, intellectual, and articulate. She knew many of the movers and shakers of the early twentieth century: agitators, intellectuals, writers, union organizers, and even First Lady Eleanor Roosevelt. She was a journalist, pacifist, radical, mother, voice for legions of the voiceless, daily reader of Scripture, marcher with strikers and suffragettes, and provider of thousands of bowls of soup. She valued her principles highly enough to go to jail for them.

But above all, Dorothy Day was a Catholic, living a radical life rooted in the radical gospel of Jesus Christ.

One of most influential women of the twentieth century, Dorothy Day awakened the conscience of her country and her church to the plight of the hungry, homeless, and helpless people who lived in the nation's shadows. Through Dorothy's passion for justice, the *Catholic Worker* newspaper and movement she started with Peter Maurin in 1933 had an incalculable influence on American society and the Catholic Church. Still in publication today, *The Catholic Worker* continues to sell for a penny a copy.

There are approximately 185 Catholic Worker "hospitality homes" for poor people around the world; homes which continue to feed and shelter thousands. The integrity and principled stands of the Catholic Worker movement have motivated countless people to practice the works of mercy. Pragmatic and contemplative, Dorothy Day, as both writer and written about, has left us a treasury of inspired spiritual writing which gives us a glimpse into her soul.

When faced with the dilemma that all justice-seekers face—work to effect systemic change or meet the needs of the person at your door—Dorothy Day did both. And as she met the needs and healed the wounds of others, she also applied the soothing balm of grace to her own soul. For much of her early life, only barely realizing it, Dorothy searched for God. Through helping to heal the material needs of people who were desperately poor, her "long loneliness," was finally eased by her conversion to Catholicism after a long search for God.

Background
In Dorothy Day's time, she witnessed dramatic change—the inventions of the automobile and television, two world wars, the struggles of workers to unionize, and two revolutions for women—the first one in the 1920s, which liberated women and ultimately led to their right to vote, and the second one, popularly known as the "sexual revolution" in the 1960s. One of five children, she spent her childhood in Chicago, where her father worked as a journalist. Dorothy attended the University of Illinois on a scholarship and was particularly interested in the political writings of her day.

When her father got a job in New York in 1916, Dorothy moved there with her family. While she had been aware of the poverty in Chicago, the poverty she witnessed in New York was on a greater scale, and she was appalled by the smells, filth, and sprawl of the tenements. From the age of twenty, her desire to live among God's poor was intertwined with her journey with God.

Dorothy became a journalist, working for various newspapers. She covered peace movements; labor organizing efforts; and the struggles of the desperately poor. She wanted to be alongside the workers on the picket lines, to fight for them, to write about them, and as she often said, "make her mark" on the world.

But with her work alongside the workers in picket lines and the suffragettes demonstrating for the right to vote came jail. And, go to jail she did. The first of her several times in jail was when she joined the suffragettes in Washington in 1917. In a dank, unheated cell by herself, the young Dorothy Day had ample time to reflect on the human condition. It was in that jail that she realized that up until that point she had a lot of theoretical knowledge about injustice and hunger, but she had not experienced it firsthand until that day. She was no longer satisfied to simply write about others' problems, she wanted to be more actively engaged. And so the journalist became an activist.

Dorothy spent several years living a fast-paced bohemian lifestyle in Greenwich Village in the early 1920s, in the company of not-as-yet-known writers like John Dos Passos, Malcolm Cowley, and her good friend Eugene O'Neill. Twenty years later, in interviews with author Robert Coles, Dorothy reflected on her efforts to forget her years in Greenwich Village:

> When I finished writing about them in *The Long Loneliness,* I thought I was through with them, but we're never through with our lives I've begun to realize—any part of them.... I was foolish then; I was caught in stormy love affairs or infatuations; there is no other way to put it.[1]

One of these love affairs was with Forster Batterham, who shared Dorothy's political views but was also a confirmed atheist. Very much in love and living in a common-law marriage, Dorothy became pregnant with their daughter. With the birth and baptism of Tamar Teresa, Day finally acquiesced to God—the "hound of heaven" who had been chasing her all her life. The God she had been wrestling with through the years now triumphed.

Knowing that her own baptism as a Catholic would mean losing the man she deeply loved, Day still chose to be baptized into the Catholic Church. She recognized however, that her baptism was just another step on the spiritual journey that had begun on the pavement and in the bars of New York. Reflecting on these early years in the church, Dorothy recalled: "I thought of myself—well, not as a Catholic convert. I thought of myself as someone who had been looking for God all those years, without really knowing it, and had now *begun* to find Him, but who had a long way to go: 'the long loneliness.'"[2]

As Fr. James Martin points out in *My Life with the Saints*, becoming a Catholic synthesized Dorothy's ideals in life: "The Catholic Church bound together Dorothy's love for the poor, her desire to be in communion with God, her search for moral clarity, and her hope for a life of humility and obedience."[3] Dorothy continued to heal her "long loneliness" by advocating for people who were closest to her heart—God's poor.

The Catholic magazine *Commonweal* commissioned Dorothy to travel to Washington, D.C., to cover the hunger marches of 1932. Millions of Americans, jobless, homeless, and without food, marched to ask their government for assistance. Although years later the programs they marched for were enacted, Congress and the Hoover administration roughly rebuffed the protesters. As she watched, Dorothy realized that her Catholic Church was not where she expected it to be—marching with the poor. The church certainly dispensed a great deal of charity, she admitted, but she felt that the church didn't address the social problems that caused poverty and the necessity of charity in the first place.

As the works of mercy seemed to Dorothy to be a crucial part of Catholic doctrine, she could not understand why well-off people ignored the poor:

> I remember, after the Depression began, seeing hundreds of people on the street, begging and hungry and with a look of sadness in their faces that made me want to cry. Then I would see well-dressed people coming out of Manhattan churches...as complacent as could be in their conviction that God was theirs....[4]

After one of the hunger marches, Dorothy made her way to the Shrine of the Immaculate Conception on the feast of the Immaculate Conception. She knelt, prayed, and cried and asked God to help her use her talents to help the poor and working class.

It did not take long for her prayer to be answered.

Peter Arrives

There are moments when two people meet that the grace from the spiritual bond they form flows far beyond them to touch countless others. One thinks of Francis and Clare, John of the Cross and Teresa of Avila, Francis DeSales and Jane de Chantal. Such a moment occurred when Dorothy returned from the hunger marches to find a short, stocky, rugged man in his mid-fifties. His name was Peter Maurin.

"Peter's arrival changed everything, everything.... I finally found a purpose in my life and the teacher I needed."[5] Peter Maurin, called "peasant of the pavements" by Dorothy, was from a large Catholic family in France. A Salesian brother for a short time, he had taught school briefly before coming to America. He was a philosopher and a devout Catholic and stood firmly with the poor. He had been influenced by Pope Leo XIII's encyclical of 1891, *Rerum Novarum,* which calls Catholics to exercise a "preferential option for the poor." Peter and Dorothy became friends, colleagues, mentors for one another, and soul mates.

Peter's influence on Dorothy was profound. Although baptized, Dorothy had received little instruction about Catholicism's teachings and doctrine. Peter taught her about papal encyclicals, the social teaching of the Catholic Church, and its rich traditions, like the communion of saints. His personal mission was to live like Jesus and to make the "encyclicals click." Because he emphasized seeing Christ in every person, Peter wanted to build a new society in which all were equal.

Dorothy received his instruction eagerly. She was heartened to hear the church's emphasis on the preferential option for the poor. She was encouraged by the stories of the women saints like Teresa of Avila and Catherine of Siena, both of whom challenged church authority. In *Dorothy Day: A Radical Devotion* Robert Coles explains how Peter, speaking of Catherine of Siena, declared: "'Ah, there was a saint who had an influence on her times.' Then he plunged into a discussion of Saint Catherine's letters to the popes and other public figures of the fourteenth century, in which she took them to task for their failings."[6]

The Catholic Worker

The Letter to the Hebrews makes it clear that welcoming others is a sacred duty: "Do not neglect to show hospitality to strangers, for by doing that some have entertained angels without knowing it" (Hebrews 13:2). Peter had firm convictions about offering hospitality to others, especially those in need, Dorothy recalls "Peter Maurin spoke to me often of his ideas about hospitality, a concept I understand well because I had lived so long on the Lower East Side of New York—and the poor are noted for their hospitality."[7]

At Peter's suggestion, they published a newspaper, bringing together Dorothy's writing ability and Peter's philosophy of the common good. *The Catholic Worker* contained articles by both Dorothy and Peter, explaining their philosophy in light of Catholic social justice teaching. Their first edition, issued in May 1933 sold out its 25,000 copies. Circulation soon increased to 100,000 and then to 150,000 by 1936.

The timing of the publication of *The Catholic Worker* was perfect. It was the height of the Great Depression, and millions of Americans were suffering. The justice-oriented newspaper was a phenomenal success: Parishes throughout the nation subscribed in huge numbers. Peter Maurin used his "Easy Essays" to present his philosophy of advancing the common good and the equality of all people. Dorothy wrote columns (which continue to be reprinted today) about contemporary issues that gave hope to some and pricked the consciences of others.

Practicing what they preached about the works of mercy, Dorothy and Peter opened "hospitality houses" for the homeless. Dorothy recalled the urgency of the situation: "Peter and I saw those people standing at corners, or sitting on park benches, and we felt that something *had* to be done, and right away."[8] Others joined them, giving up careers in order to live the Gospel and perform the works of mercy. Gradually, what was never intended to be a movement turned into one—one that touched countless lives, both the people who came to be served, and the people who did the serving.

One of those volunteers whose life was changed by the Catholic Worker movement is Sr. Mary Elizabeth Clark, S.S.J. In the 1970s Mary Elizabeth was a missioner in a wealthy parish in northern New Jersey. Having grown up in a "sheltered suburban situation," Mary Elizabeth, feeling a need to touch and be touched by the poor, invited Catholic Workers to her parish to speak. One day one of them returned the invitation, asking Sr. Mary Elizabeth to come to her Catholic Worker house. She spent several summers helping out at Mary House on Third Street, where Dorothy Day lived:

> It was hard at first, the smell of unclean bodies, and sleeping on a mattress on the floor with vermin running around, but it was also a transformative time for me. I saw the suffering Jesus in the stark life of the women who came there and the healing Jesus in the loving service that surrounded them. I ate it up and decided to devote my life to advocate for marginalized people.[9]

It is this notion of "call," of dedication, that is one difference between Catholic Worker houses and "homeless shelters." There are no distinctions between staff and guests at Catholic Worker homes; everyone is equal.

Sr. Mary Elizabeth describes Dorothy Day as humble, never allowing herself to be put on a pedestal. This spirit of humility included an emphasis on faith and prayer. Dorothy set the tone, living right alongside the guests, wearing the same clothing that was available to them, thereby sending the message that always, in all ways, everyone was equal in a Catholic Worker hospitality house.

This lack of distinction between server and served is truly important when working with marginalized people. It stresses commonality rather than difference; it fosters dignity and respect. As St. Damien's life indicated, there is no greater gift to give someone in need than simple presence, a willingness to be with them no matter what. It tells people that whatever their life condition, there are others who care enough about them to share their lives. This can go a long way toward healing the deep woundedness and rejection that often accompany a life lived in the shadows of society.

Pacifism

Dorothy and Peter believed that war was murder, that it was simply not compatible with a religion that stressed love. Their stance cost *The Catholic Worker* a great deal in terms of lost readership, especially during World War II. Despite the fierce opposition, they held their ground, stating, "Lots of Catholics were angry at us when we maintained our pacifism, with agony, during the Second World War. Lots of Catholics were angry when we weren't running to build bomb shelters in the 1950s, when we protested the madness of bomb shelters in a nuclear age, the madness of war in *any* age."[10]

Although Dorothy and Peter were confirmed pacifists, they had made it a point to warn their readers about the evils of fascism and advised their readers to oppose Hitler. Despite being arrested several times in the 1950s for anti-nuclear protests, Dorothy maintained until her death her conviction that war was not compatible with the Gospel of Jesus.

Duty of Delight

As Robert Ellsberg points out in his article about Dorothy Day's diaries, "The Duty of Delight," he points out that this rather unusual phrase appears often in Dorothy's diary entries.[11] Probably most of us do not "delight" in all of our duties, all of the time. Did Dorothy feel the same? What did "the duty of delight" mean to her? An interior attitude to find a measure of joy in even the most onerous tasks? To constantly radiate happiness in any and all situations?

It may have been all of these and even more: Ellsberg explains that this phrase was "a refrain" for Dorothy and it explained an attitude that ran throughout her writing. For example, Ellsberg notes, Dorothy often expressed the conviction "that love is not a feeling but a matter of the will."[12] In an echo of the adage, "Fake it till you make it," Dorothy tried to act lovingly even when not feeling very loving in her heart. She was clear that one could will to love even difficult people by trying hard enough: "If you will to love someone, you soon do.... It depends on how hard you try."[13]

Certainly this is a different perspective on love from how "love" is viewed in popular culture—that soft, warm feeling of romantic love that is portrayed in music and on television. Deliberately choosing to act in a loving manner toward someone we find difficult is a matter of choice. Depending on the situation, it may even be considered heroic virtue. It certainly is one way we can follow in the footsteps of Dorothy Day.

"Don't Call Me a Saint"

It is easy to misinterpret this famous saying of Dorothy Day's. Certainly, true to her humility, she never sought the spotlight or any credit for the tremendous impact she had on the American Catholic Church. However, it is also clear that calling her a "saint" and placing her on a pedestal distances her from the rest of us, mistakenly conveying the impression that only someone as "special" as Dorothy can live and work with poor people. Despite this, however, Cardinal John O'Connor of New York submitted Dorothy's cause for canonization to the Vatican in 2000. The Vatican approved her cause, bestowing on her the title "Servant of God." Whether or not she is ever formally canonized, Dorothy Day is already canonized in the hearts of the thousands of people she inspired to work for justice for all.

Reflection

I first heard of Dorothy Day on the day she died, during a conversation with some Sister of St. Joseph at St. Maria Goretti High School, where I taught English in South Philadelphia. Little did I suspect at that moment how I would eventually come to admire and respect this woman, Dorothy Day.

Although born and raised in a Catholic environment, I went through a period of questioning my faith in my twenties. I lived in Center City Philadelphia, where, like Dorothy Day, I enthusiastically participated in the nightlife and the cultural opportunities of a great city. While on one level I enjoyed myself, on a deeper level I was going through a faith crisis, wondering why God would allow such horrors as the bombing of children during the Vietnam War. Being diagnosed with rheumatoid arthritis drew me even further away from God and the church. I lived in "Why me, God?" mode for several years.

God, of course, never gave up on me, slowly, gently drawing me back. After taking a summer course in spirituality and praying the Gospels as the radical documents they are, I felt a call to give myself completely to God in religious life.

Like the narrator of Francis Thompson's "The Hound of Heaven," I respectfully refused God's invitation for a few years. As Dorothy's story shows, though, when God wants you, God gets you. I entered the Sisters of St. Joseph of Chestnut Hill, Philadelphia, in 1983. My ministry has long been advocating for the civil rights of the disability community. Like Dorothy Day, I have marched in protests in Washington, D.C., although with one difference: I roll along in a long line of people in wheelchairs. Our goal is to increase disability rights regarding accessible housing, employment, and living where we want. With her strong emphasis on the dignity of every human person, I know Dorothy would be with us if she were still alive.

I pray to follow Dorothy's example: to see Christ in every person, to try to live as simply as possible, and to advocate for justice. Although it is difficult, I attempt to make choices mindful of the people who are poor. The disabled people I stand with are too often demeaned, devalued, dismissed, denied basic choices in life that others take for granted. I am convinced, though, that Jesus is with us in this struggle for human dignity. And I have a feeling that Dorothy Day and Peter Maurin approve.

CHAPTER EIGHT

BLESSED MOTHER TERESA OF CALCUTTA
(1910–1997)
Healing in the Slums of Calcutta

Mother Teresa of Calcutta and her visiting friend, Sr. Anastasia Hearne, S.S.J., (a fellow sister of mine) were on their way to Bangladesh when Mother Teresa told the driver to stop and asked Sr. Anastasia to retrieve a brown paper bag sitting in the midst of garbage. Sr. Anastasia picked up the bag and was shocked to find a baby inside. Startled, she asked Mother Teresa: "How did you know there was a child in this bag?" "Because," Mother Teresa replied, "no one in India would throw out something as precious as a brown bag."

On the night of September 5, 1997, the lights in Calcutta, India, went out due to an electrical failure. That power outage extinguished a far brighter light that night, as Mother Teresa of Calcutta drew her last breath when her breathing apparatus failed to function.

An exceedingly humble woman, Agnes Gonxha Bojaxhiu, later known as Mother Teresa, neither sought nor welcomed the fame and public esteem bestowed on her in life. (As of this writing, Mother Teresa is now Blessed Teresa of Calcutta; however, I will refer to her by her more familiar name, Mother Teresa.)

Her story is well known: Agnes Gonxha Bojaxhiu was born in 1910 in Skopje, a small town in Albania. Always wanting to be a missionary, she entered the Sisters of Loreto of Ireland in 1928 at the age of eighteen; she chose the name "Teresa" in honor of the recently canonized St. Thérèse of Lisieux. While still a novice, she was sent to India as a teacher in a boarding school for upper-class young women. A hard worker, she poured herself into her ministry, often teaching many grade levels at the same time. After being appointed principal in 1944, Mother Teresa risked her life at one point by leaving the convent school during a riot in order to procure some food.

Mother Teresa was quite happy teaching in the convent school. However, the extreme poverty in the slums of Calcutta deeply disturbed her. In September 1946, on her way to a retreat in Darjeeling, Mother Teresa had a profound mystical experience. Although she was always reticent about recounting the precise details of this encounter with God, like St. Damien of Molokai, Mother Teresa received her own "call within a call": "It was in that train, I heard the call to give up all and follow Him into the slums—to serve Him in the poorest of the poor."[1] Thus began the Congregation of the Missionaries of Charity, whose goal was expressed by Mother Teresa as: "The General End of the Missionaries of Charity is to satiate the thirst of Jesus Christ on the cross for Love and Souls."[2]

Realizing that her life with the Sisters of Loretto would not fulfill this new call from God, she set out, like St. Teresa of Avila, on the challenging task of founding a new congregation. Mother Teresa's two-year struggle to establish her new community was quite similar to Teresa of Avila's endeavor: Both had to secure many permissions, extract themselves from their present communities, and find a suitable house for a convent. They also both encountered considerable human resistance while listening to a divine voice.

Initially, Archbishop Ferdinand Périer of Calcutta had many reservations about this new congregation: Where would new sisters come from? What exactly would this new community do? Mother Teresa explained her vision in detail: She wanted native Indian nuns to live and work among their own poor, ill, destitute, and dying people. Women from other countries would be welcome to join as long as they would live a lifestyle of radical poverty: "We have to be very very poor in every sense of the word to gain the heart of the poor for Christ," she insisted.[3]

After many months of determined pleading, Mother Teresa finally received permission from Archbishop Périer to proceed with her plans. With that authorization granted, and with the blessing of the Mother General of the Sisters of Loreto, Mother Teresa left the Loreto convent in a sari, with only five rupees to her name. After a few months of studying basic nursing practices, Mother Teresa was ready to embark on a new life of ministering with impoverished people.

On December 12, 1948, Mother Teresa of Calcutta went into the slums of that city for the first time as a Missionary of Charity. Calcutta was a city of contrasts: beautiful palaces for the wealthy, slums for the poor. Destitute people lived on the streets, or in tiny shacks if they were lucky; food was scarce; medical care non-existent.

"Slum Sister"

Initially Mother Teresa was criticized for working with poor rather than rich people, and was referred to as the "Slum Sister." She rebutted this criticism by pointing out that the wealthy already had many priests and nuns ministering to them—why not bring God to the lowest of the low in Indian society? She had had a taste of their poverty herself, as she spent several weeks without a home until she acquired her first convent.

> *One night in 1973, Mother Teresa received a phone call at 2 AM On the other end was Sr. Anastasia, S.S.J., an administrator for the Human Relations Commission of the Archdiocese of Philadelphia. "Sister, do you know what time it is here in Calcutta?" asked the deep voice of Mother Teresa. Sr. Anastasia confessed that, in her eagerness to invite Mother Teresa to speak at a peace rally in Philadelphia, she had not been aware that she was calling India in the middle of their night. "Send me your request in writing," Mother Teresa said, "and I'll respond to it." She not only responded, but gave an inspiring talk at the peace rally on Philadelphia's Benjamin Franklin Parkway. That was the beginning of their friendship.*

As with Henriette Delille a century earlier in New Orleans, Mother Teresa's radical poverty and charismatic personality soon attracted young women to join her. Some were her former students from the Loreto convent school; others heard about her mission and asked to enter the Missionaries of Charity. On October 7, 1950, Archbishop Périer officially established the Missionaries of Charity as a religious community in the diocese of Calcutta. People who were unloved, unwanted, and uncared for now began to receive needed love, care, and prayer.

Spiritual Darkness

As we have seen, the inspiration for the Missionaries of Charity came to Mother Teresa while she was traveling to her annual retreat in September 1946. Although she rarely spoke of it in detail, it was apparent that she had experienced a profound, mystical union with Christ, a union which provided her with deep consolation and ecstatic joy.

Every mystic has written about the difficulty of describing this mystical union; it simply cannot be expressed in human language. We can try to prepare for it by personal prayer and sacrifice, reception of the sacraments, and asking God for the grace of this ecstatic union. We cannot however, insist that God grant this mystical experience; it is always pure gift from God.

Even before Mother Teresa's mystical experience, her daily prayer life had brought her into a close relationship with God. In order to understand the great pain of her subsequent spiritual darkness, it is important to know how deeply in love with God she was. We cannot miss something that we have never had.

In *Come, Be My Light*, Missionaries of Charity Fr. Brian Kolodiejchuk describes what spiritual darkness meant for Mother Teresa: "...the term would come to signify profound interior suffering, lack of sensible consolation, spiritual dryness, an apparent absence of God from her life, and, at the same time, a painful longing for Him."[4] Ironically, this spiritual darkness began at the exact time that Mother Teresa started her ministry in the slums of Calcutta. It lasted for decades. Virtually no one knew about it, as Mother Teresa only shared her pain with her spiritual directors.

And it certainly was a deep darkness. In 1955, after telling Archbishop Perier about her darkness and longing for God, he tried to console Mother Teresa by pointing out that many great saints, including her patron Thérèse of Lisieux, also experienced deep darkness. He referred to *The Dark Night of the Soul*, the mystical classic by St. John of the Cross, which teaches that spiritual desolation, painful as it is, eventually leads to spiritual maturity and union with God. Mother Teresa, apparently not consoled by his words, responded: "Pray for me—for within me everything is icy cold. It is only that blind faith that carries me through for in reality to me all is darkness."[5]

It initially can be shocking to learn that the world-famous Mother Teresa, renowned as an icon of holiness and goodness, lived with spiritual darkness. This reminds us, however, that even saints have spiritual struggles, that when we have our own feelings of abandonment by God, Mother Teresa of Calcutta experienced this also. God's mysterious ways are certainly not our ways; we are far too limited to understand the mind of God. Just as seeds germinate in the darkness of the earth, God uses spiritual darkness to bring spiritual light. Mother Teresa's seeming separation from God never kept her from bringing others, especially the poor in the "dark holes," to the light of goodness and God.

> *Later, it was Mother Teresa making the request. She called Sr. Anastasia and told her, "Babies are dying in the bush." She then explained that she possessed the necessary ingredients to make a life-sustaining formula for infants in rural areas, but she did not know the exact measurements. Sr. Anastasia answered, "But Mother, I don't know anything about baby formula." "Well, learn, Sister, learn," was the reply.*
>
> *So, with the help of nutritionists in Philadelphia, Sr. Anastasia learned how to mix the exact portions of the infant formula. She called Mother Teresa to tell her that she would send the instructions; Mother Teresa, however,*

*wanted a bit more than just the instructions. She wanted
Sr. Anastasia herself to come to India to teach the mothers: "They will listen to you because you are a sister."*

*So, Sr. Anastasia journeyed to India to train the mothers
to use the proper measurements for the infant formula.
The results were astounding: Every infant gained weight.
Mother dubbed the formula "St. Joseph's" in honor of Sr.
Anastasia's community.*

"Dark Holes"

Despite her inner darkness, Mother Teresa remained committed to
her ministry with very poor people in Calcutta. It was there that
she came closest to God: "[W]hen I walk through the slums or
enter the dark holes—there Our Lord is really present."[6] There was
a paradox in her soul: on the one hand a profound longing for
Jesus, yet not being able to experience him as she had before. Since
she found Jesus in people who were very poor, her darkness
increased her already radical missionary zeal. This zeal was conta-
gious. Since its foundation, the Missionaries of Charity have flourished, with over four thousand sisters in foundations all over the
world, including many in the United States. There are also
Missionaries of Charity brothers and priests.

Even as Mother Teresa lived with her cauldron of inner pain, the
local media in Calcutta began to recognize and praise her work. As
we might expect, Mother Teresa had no interest in becoming
famous; fame was thrust upon her as the public became aware of
her ministry.

One man who did a great deal to increase public awareness of
Mother Teresa was Malcolm Muggeridge, a well-known British
author and commentator. He was so deeply impressed by Mother
Teresa that in 1971 he wrote a book entitled *Something Beautiful*

for God, in which he says of her, "I never met anyone more memorable."[7] He also recounts an anecdote from his time with Mother
Teresa: "Once I had occasion to see her off, with one of the Sisters,
at Calcutta railway station.... When the train began to move, and
I walked away, I felt as though I were leaving behind me all the
beauty and all the joy in the universe."[8]

> *On another occasion, Sr. Anastasia accompanied Mother
> Teresa on a visit to a hospital for people with leprosy.
> Mother Teresa, completely unconcerned about the conta-
> gious aspect of the disease, went to people, touching them
> and blessing them. Sensing Sr. Anastasia's apprehension,
> Mother invited her to do the same. She complied, but was
> horrified when one man's leg fell off from the knee down.
> None of the workers however, showed any surprise, as
> limbs falling off was a common occurrence with people
> with leprosy.*

While she brought joy to others, no one ever suspected the interior
desolation in Mother Teresa's heart. She covered her inner suffering with a perpetual smile, and admonished her sisters to do the
same, for if they seemed unhappy, they could make the people they
ministered with unhappy.

Fr. Joseph Neuner, a Jesuit priest, became Mother Teresa's spiritual director in the late 1950s. He proved to be exceedingly help-
ful to her, inviting her not only to accept, but to love the darkness
of her heart. It was a great grace to learn that *it was her darkness
itself* that united her with the passion of Jesus: "...I have come to
love the darkness. —For I believe now that it is a part, a very very
small part of Jesus' darkness & pain on earth."[9] Fr. Neuner also
pointed out that her spiritual darkness was her unique suffering,
the suffering that connected her with the poor people whom she
loved so much.

Who Is Hungry?

Sr. Eileen Side, S.S.J., attended an impromptu talk given by Mother Teresa at the Eucharistic Congress in Philadelphia in 1976. Mother Teresa returned again and again to one simple question, "Who in your house is hungry?"[10] Upon first hearing it, Sr. Eileen naturally thought to herself that no one in her house was hungry. After Mother Teresa said it for the third time, Sr. Eileen realized that Mother Teresa was referring to a much deeper hunger. With all her experience in developing countries like India, Mother Teresa realized that people in wealthy nations also are hungry. Theirs is a different type of hunger, a spiritual hunger: larger houses and luxury SUVs do not fulfill the hunger for love, for community, and for connection with God and other people.

Yes, Mother Teresa's death extinguished her shining light, a light that had led so many to God. Hers was a light that touched millions around the world. It was a light for all of us, a light to remind us to remember our sisters and brothers who hunger in so many different ways.

Reflection

Like her patron St. Thérèse of Lisieux, Mother Teresa stressed the importance of doing small things with great love, because Christ is in every person we meet. Most of us are not called to be extraordinary leaders like Mother Teresa, but we can certainly follow her example in our daily lives.

In my own life I always wanted to be a giver, not a receiver. During my first few years of needing help from others, I struggled with my pride—I wanted to help others, not be helped. Through prayer and spiritual direction, I began to grow a bit more comfortable with asking others for assistance, finding most people willing to help. While this made it easier to ask, deep down my pride still rebelled; I resented being in this needy position.

Eventually I realized how replete with opportunities for grace my situation was. While I fervently disliked requesting help with minor tasks like opening a car door, I knew that it gave me the chance to identify with the helpless Jesus on the way to Calvary. The Fifth Station of the Cross, where Jesus allows Simon of Cyrene to carry his cross, became my spiritual rallying point. It kept me in touch with my call to imitate the humility of Jesus, and also reminded me to be grateful for the many Simons of Cyrene in my life.

As this grace deepened in me, I began to realize how important it is for all of us to hear the words "thank you." Of course we were all taught to *say* "thank you" from the time we were two years old; for most disabled or elderly people, though, especially anyone with a background in a helping profession, it is also important to *hear* "thank you." In my years of pastoral ministry with people with all types of disabilities, I learned how much we all need to be needed, to contribute to the common good in some way.

When one person helps another in whatever way, large or small, that action to me is an exchange of love. Jesus himself modeled this: He allowed himself to receive, as well as give, assistance. I believe that his example shows that *it doesn't matter which side of the exchange you are on.* Giver or receiver, that exchange of love helps to build up the grace of the Mystical Body of Christ. Every act of kindness we perform or receive contributes to the goodness in the world. I now appreciate that life is much less about rugged individualism, and much more about interdependence, that interlocking web of humanity. One of the greatest graces I have received in my years of ministering as a woman religious with a disability is the conviction that God has put us here for one another.

CHAPTER NINE

ARCHBISHOP OSCAR ROMERO
(1917–1980)
Healing El Salvador

He had just come to the end of his homily when the shots rang out. He immediately slumped to the floor, lying at the foot of the altar's crucifix. The single bullet that struck him in the chest caused heavy internal bleeding. He was rushed to a hospital, but it was too late. Oscar Romero, Archbishop of El Salvador, had been assassinated.

One of the world's most renowned human rights activists, famous worldwide as the "voice of the voiceless," now lay dead under the cross of Jesus Christ. As his friend and noted liberation theologian Jon Sobrino writes: "…Archbishop Romero's death was not like other deaths. Like the death of Jesus, it was a murder and a martyrdom."[1]

He had known for a while that it was coming. He knew he was in danger and could ultimately be murdered, because of his continued support of the *campesinos*, the farm laborers of El Salvador, and his insistence that the Salvadoran church stand up to the oligarchy of the wealthy and the right-wing government.

Oscar

The future martyr Oscar Arnulfo Romero y Galdamez was born on August 15, 1917, in Ciudad Barrios, located in the northeastern corner of El Salvador. His father, Santos, the town postmaster, often sent young Oscar to deliver telegrams and messages to others in town. Until he was twelve, Oscar studied in a one-room school with only one teacher. His father resisted Oscar's desire to go into the seminary and apprenticed him to a local carpenter. However, during a visit to Ciudad Barrios by the Vicar-General of the diocese, Oscar expressed his desire to be a priest. Shortly after, with his father's reluctant consent, Oscar left for the seminary. Oscar was an excellent student and the bishop sent him to Rome to complete his studies for ordination.

Pope Pius XI was pope during Romero's years in Rome. In a touch of foreshadowing of Romero's later life, he particularly admired Pope Pius XI for standing up and opposing fascism and Nazism. Oscar Romero was ordained in Rome in 1942, after which he returned to his native land. After serving as a parish priest for a few years, his bishop asked him to become secretary of the diocese of San Miguel. He served in this and various other priestly ministries until 1970, when he was appointed auxiliary bishop to Archbishop Chavez in San Salvador. He would be an eyewitness to the beginning of the most bitter and bloody decades in the history of El Salvador.

El Salvador

The Republic of El Salvador is the smallest and most densely populated country in Central America. Nestled between Guatemala and Honduras, El Salvador has a population of some seven million people, many of whom are Roman Catholic.

Native American peoples called the "Pipil," who were descendents of the Aztecs, settled in the region around the eleventh century. Spanish conquistador Pedro de Alvarado invaded and conquered El Salvador in the early sixteenth century. King Charles I of Spain officially proclaimed San Salvador a city in 1546. By 1821 El Salvador and other Central American countries had declared their independence from Spain. Throughout the remainder of the nineteenth and early twentieth centuries, periods of peace were punctuated by revolts of the *campesinos*, who worked the land but were not permitted to own it.

It was during the 1970s, just after Romero became auxiliary bishop in the nation's capital, that genuine civil war broke out in El Salvador. A tiny number of wealthy landowners controlled the government, the media, the military, and the rest of the population. *Campesinos* began to demand a share of the land, rather than farming it for the wealthy for a pittance. Increasingly frequent uprisings were brutally suppressed by the military.

Liberation Theology

In 1968 the Latin American bishops' conference held an important meeting at Medellín, Colombia. Its purpose was to apply the principles of Vatican II to Latin America: "Thus, for our authentic liberation, all of us need a profound conversion so that 'the kingdom of justice, love and peace,' might come to us."[2] The bishops did not hesitate to point out injustice: "Extreme inequality (exists) among social classes: especially, though not exclusively, in those countries where a few have much (culture, wealth, power, prestige) while the majority has very little."[3]

The Medellín Conference was a turning point for the Latin American church, clearly positioning it to actively advocate for the huge numbers of oppressed peoples in their countries.

In mid–twentieth century Latin America, the old saying that "the rich get richer and the poor get poorer," was all too true. Poor people were denied land, were continually exploited, and were not permitted a voice in the government. This, combined with the winds of change of modernization that had blown through the church after Vatican II, led priests and nuns to advocate for the desperately poor people with whom they ministered. Theologians, reflecting a "theology from below," interpreted the gospel message in light of the conditions of the poor, thus the term "liberation theology." The most prominent text of the movement, *A Theology of Liberation*, was written by the Peruvian priest Gustavo Gutiérrez in 1971.

Fr. James Brockman, s.j., author of *The Word Remains: The Life of Oscar Romero*, explains liberation theology:

> The basic ideas...were also embedded in the Medellín documents: that God does not will social injustice, but rather, the opposite, and that people must work and struggle with God's help to bring about justice. Such ideas immediately challenge the social order and those in power and lead to conflict in the political order.[4]

As in other parts of the world, however, many members of the church hierarchy in Latin America were slow to embrace change; some actually resisted it. Within El Salvador itself, Archbishop Luis Chavez took the principles of Medellín to heart and began to call attention to the miserable plight of the *campesinos*. Many of his bishops in other Salvadoran dioceses, however, preferred the status quo and refused to follow his lead.

For his part, Oscar Romero had never been the kind of man to make waves. He was profoundly loyal to the church and its hierarchy, and resisted much of Vatican II: "From 1962 to 1965 Romero watched as Vatican Council II began to stir the waters of the church, and he would later show that he had read and pondered its pronouncements. But he by no means sympathized with all the tendencies that appeared in the church after the council."[5] Romero referred to the documents of Medellín as a "false ideology."

When Oscar Romero was named auxiliary bishop of San Salvador, not all of the clergy were pleased:

> For some priests and others who had pondered the new direction given the church by Vatican II and the pronouncements of the Latin American bishops at Medellín in 1968, Romero still seemed wedded to the old ways and his ordination an assertion of the old triumphalism that Vatican II had renounced.[6]

Archbishop

Archbishop Luis Chavez retired in 1977. As El Salvador was a small country with only one archdiocese, the archbishop of San Salvador was the preeminent leader of the church. The Salvadoran oligarchy had never been fond of Chavez, as he was wont to point out their continual and thorough exploitation of the El Salvadoran people. The wealthy landowners pressured Emanuele Gerada, the papal nuncio, to appoint a conservative without the annoying tendencies toward social justice that Archbishop Chavez had exhibited. They wanted a new archbishop who attended church matters, minded his own business, and let the status quo remain—Bishop Romero, with his conservative and agreeable nature, was perfect for the job.[7]

On the other hand, most of the priests and religious in the country wanted a new leader in the justice mold of Archbishop Chavez. Most clergy wanted the new archbishop to be Bishop Arturo

Rivera Damas, an auxiliary of the archdiocese since 1960.[8] Ministering closely with the *campesinos*, the priests and religious of El Salvador wanted the church hierarchy to join them in fighting for their rights.

Rutilio Grande, s.j.

It was a hot sunny afternoon in Aguilares, a town just north of San Salvador. An old man, a young boy, and a Jesuit priest drove through the sugarcane field, on their way to Saturday evening Mass, unaware that they were moving toward their deaths. After the machine guns had done their work, the three lay dead under the hot Salvadoran sun. Their murders became the catalyst that stirred the soul of Oscar Romero, newly consecrated archbishop of El Salvador.

Rutilio Grande, s.j., and Oscar Romero were friends. They had met when Romero was living at the Jesuit-run seminary where Grande was rector. Fr. Grande was highly regarded in El Salvador for speaking out on behalf of the *campesinos*. Pastor of the church in Aguilares, Fr. Grande was supervising a group of young Jesuits in establishing *comunidads de base*, or small Christian communities, in order to organize and empower the *campesinos* through reading and understanding Scripture. The wealthy landowners were not at all pleased with the peasants' organizing nor with how Fr. Rutilio Grande used his sermons to denounce the injustice of a few dominating and exploiting the many.[9]

Romero had such respect for his friend Rutilio Grande that he invited him to be master of ceremonies at his consecration as bishop. However, Romero did not agree with Fr. Grande's attempts to confront the oligarchy: "He did not...approve of Rutilio's pastoral ministry at Aquilares. It seemed too political to him, too horizontal, foreign to the church's basic mission, and dangerously close to revolutionary ideas."[10] Despite these reservations, Romero knew that Grande was a faithful and prayerful priest, and loved him as a friend.

Radical Change

The assassination of his good friend Rutilio Grande changed Oscar Romero profoundly. He had been archbishop for only three months and had tried to accommodate himself to the demands of the oligarchy as best he could. Certainly no fool, Romero knew the powers in the country had expected him to keep a low profile. In Jon Sobrino's *Archbishop Romero: Memories and Reflections*, Sobrino noted Romero's change:

> Archbishop Romero was altogether aware, from the out-set, that he had been the candidate of the right.... They would build him a magnificent bishop's palace, they told him, and they hoped he would reverse the line taken by his predecessor Luis Chávez y Gonzáles. But Archbishop Romero changed, and changed radically.[11]

What the landowners had failed to realize was that, along with his conservative views, their new archbishop firmly believed in the message of the gospel of Jesus Christ, as well as the social teachings of the Catholic Church. Having his priest friend killed in cold blood was a heavy blow, ultimately a life-changing blow. At the age of fifty-nine Archbishop Romero would never again be capable of separating God from the poor.[12] To the dismay of the members of the oligarchy, Romero fought for the rights of the poor people of El Salvador until his own murder.

Right away, Oscar Romero set the tone for the rest of his tenure, declaring that the church stood unequivocally with people who were poor. Fr. Sobrino writes: "During these same first days he published a series of communiqués denouncing the repression of the people and the persecution of the church, demanding the government investigate the murders, and promising the people that the church would be on their side."[13] To make his point clear, Romero made a public promise to never participate in any official government function until Grande's murderers were brought to justice. It was a promise that he kept.

Power never gives itself up voluntarily. It generally involves a lengthy struggle between oppressor and oppressed. In El Salvador in the late 1970s, this was more than true. The wealthy landowners had a tight grip on the country and were not about to let go easily, no matter what their new archbishop said or did.

Romero's tenure as archbishop of El Salvador was only three years long. It was marked by continual, bloody conflict between government forces and the *campesinos*; by mischaracterization of the church as "leftist" by the oligarchy; and by dissension within the church itself, especially among the bishops. As deeply as he was hated by the wealthy, Romero was as deeply loved by his people and priests.

As El Salvadoran priests began publicly calling on the oligarchy to stop murdering and repressing the *campesinos*, the government militia began killing them. A propaganda campaign was launched against the church calling it "leftist" and "Marxist." This was precisely what happened to Dorothy Day when she sided with the United Farm Workers and César Chávez in the 1960s. It is all too convenient to label as "leftist" people who stand with their poverty-stricken brothers and sisters. Eventually leftist guerillas did organize and began striking back at the right-wing militia. Romero advised his priests to condemn violence from both sides, saying, "The Christian is pacific and is not ashamed to be."[14]

The government-run newspapers and television stations continually spread propaganda about the church's actions and motivations and attempted to portray the Catholic Church as divided into two factions: the loyal faithful on one side and the so-called "radicals" who supported the poor on the other side. To counter this propaganda, the archdiocesan radio station YSAX broadcast Archbishop Romero's homilies to the nation, enabling Romero to rebut the vicious attacks with the truth.

The most painful aspect of the campaign to undermine his authority was the hostility of most of his fellow bishops. After a particularly painful meeting, Romero recalled, "[feeling] embittered about my relationship with the bishops' conference, since their personal dislike of me is obvious...."[15] Romero also struggled with Emanuele Girardi, the papal nuncio, who was not pleased with Romero's stance for the poor. His reports to the Vatican about Romero were not favorable. Archbishop Romero grew increasingly disillusioned with the Church he loved. Fr. Sobrino writes about Romero's disillusionment with the church he loved: "It was extremely painful to him that with his country screaming in agony and the priests being murdered, the Church institution offered him not support but opposition."[16]

Faith and Politics

When Jesus said, "Prophets are not without honor except in their own country and in their own house" (Matthew 13:57), he captured perfectly how Oscar must have felt—unappreciated and misunderstood in his own country. Ironically, although experiencing slanderous attacks and death threats at home, Romero was regarded with great esteem around the world: The British Parliament nominated him for a Nobel Peace Prize; foreign journalists frequently came to interview him; in February 1980, shortly before his death, the highly regarded University of Louvain in Belgium conferred an honorary doctoral degree on him. In his acceptance speech, Romero gave his view of the age-old tension between religion and politics:

> In summary I talked about what faith can do in the area of politics, the task of our archdiocese in its commitment to the country and, in the second part, how our faith becomes enormous, the mysteries become deeper through these same political realities when we are conscious of the preferential option for the poor.[17]

How difficult it is to genuinely live this message that is at the heart of the Gospel! This was the struggle in Romero's time in El Salvador—heeding the call of Christ in the Beatitudes to demand that all people deserve human rights. At one particularly tense point after several priests had been murdered, Archbishop Romero opened his homily with the following: "I have the job of picking up the trampled, the corpses and all that persecution of the church dumps along the road on its way through."[18] This was Romero's healing ministry: to mend broken bodies and spirits and comfort the bereaved. It is also a tragic yet accurate description of his priestly ministry in his own country.

El Prophete

In the first months of 1980, the death threats against Oscar Romero intensified. Repression increased, with entire *campesino* families, including children, being murdered. Romero preached a homily on March 23 addressed to all sides of the conflict, concluding with a special appeal to the army and police: "Brothers, you are part of our own people.... You kill your own campesino brothers and sisters. And before an order to kill that a man may give, the law of God must prevail that says: Thou shalt not kill! ...Stop the repression!"[19] Thunderous applause rang through the San Salvador basilica.

The next day, Monday, March 24, the archbishop went to see his confessor, then to say an evening Mass in the chapel of the Divine Providence Hospital where he lived. He preached on John's Gospel: "Very truly, I tell you, unless a grain of wheat falls into the earth and dies, it remains just a single grain; but if it dies, it bears much fruit "(John 12:24). He stated in his homily "...one must not love oneself so much as to avoid getting involved in the risks of life that history demands of us..."[20] Within minutes, the risks of his own life culminated in his death, as the bullets struck him down.

Oscar Romero's assassination stunned not only El Salvador, but also the world. Many foreign governments condemned the assassination; journalists from around the world poured into the country to cover the funeral, as did bishops to concelebrate his funeral liturgy. *Campesinos* were grief-stricken beyond words, as their champion was now gone. Government-run television stations continued their usual programming as though nothing had happened.

The violence that plagued El Salvador during his bishopric and his final Mass continued at Romero's funeral. After a bomb exploded in the corner of the cathedral, people inside and outside the church started to run, with many being trampled to death in the rush. Romero's body was hastily buried. Just as in the Mass where he was shot, Oscar Romero's funeral liturgy was never completed.

Romero's death intensified an already bloody civil war that continued until 1992, when the government and the leftist guerillas signed a peace treaty. The death toll in the war reached 75,000, including the conservative, traditionalist, priest-turned–human rights activist Oscar Romero, El Salvador's voice of the voiceless.

As of this writing, the Vatican is exploring the canonization of this man who followed his conscience and lived the Gospel. He could do no less.

Reflection

Chosen because he was theologically conservative, Oscar Romero was considered a safe bet to preserve the status quo in El Salvador. While he was not a man to rock the boat, he was also a man of the gospel. He was not able to stomach the terrible injustices being done to the poorest of his parishioners, the *campesinos*. They were the ones who performed the hard labor in the fields; they were also the ones who received virtually nothing in return for their work.

Most countries, including the United States, have their own *campesinos*, or farmworkers. In the United States, most farmworkers are migrants, moving with the harvest around the country. I once had an opportunity to minister with migrant workers and get to know their lifestyle firsthand. It was an eye-opening experience.

Shortly before I entered the Sisters of St. Joseph, I answered an ad in a Catholic newspaper seeking volunteers to work with migrant workers in North Carolina. Having recently become aware of the radical message of the Gospel of Jesus, I wanted to do whatever I could with people who were poor. I applied for the program, was accepted, and drove to a small community just outside of Raleigh, North Carolina.

There I joined a group of about twenty volunteers. I lived in a trailer with three other women, all members of different religious communities. We prayed and ate together. It was a fine experience with wonderful women.

The conditions for the farmworkers, however, were hardly wonderful. They worked long hours in blistering heat and humidity for low wages. The three distinct ethnic groups—African Americans,

Latinos, and Haitians—picked cucumbers and cut tobacco leaves, which required working in a stooped position all day. They slept in concrete bunkers and worked for crew bosses, who regarded us "religious people" with suspicion, as they did not want the conditions of the labor camps to be observed.

As I still retained a bit of my high school French, the language from which Haitian Creole is partly derived, I worked primarily with the Haitian people. Our Haitian migrants, like all farm workers, were poor and vulnerable, but they had deep faith. Often, they returned from days of back-breaking labor in the fields singing songs of praise to God.

We held Bible school for the children and prayer services for the adults. Our priest would say Mass in Creole, with much singing of joyful hymns. As the crops were drenched with toxic pesticides, sometimes migrants became ill. We took sick farm workers to the health clinic in town, always a daylong trip for even the most basic medical care. As one of my coworkers succinctly observed, "The poor must wait."

The Catholic Church's social teaching emphasizes the sacredness of life and the common good. The U.S. Catholic Bishops' Conference website notes that a basic moral test of a society is how it treats its poor and marginalized people. An important part of the church's insistent stance on the sacredness of human life, Catholic social teaching emphasizes the dignity of work, decent and fair wages, and the right of workers to unionize. This is why the bishops' Catholic Campaign for Human Development provides funding for empowerment for migrant workers in their struggle for a fair wage and improved working conditions.

Although it was some time ago, I still have vivid memories of my summer with the American *campesinos*. It is heart-wrenching to think that their lives have not improved much. Since then, when I sit down to a meal, I offer gratitude to God for the food on my plate and pray for the farm worker who helped to get it there.

CHAPTER TEN

FR. MYCHAL JUDGE
(1933–2001)
Healing with Heroism

While others ran for their lives out of the building, he ran into it, accompanying his beloved firemen. When he arrived at the World Trade Center, the horror of the scene was beyond description: clouds of orange flame billowing from the middle of the North Tower, unbreatheable smoke everywhere, and, worst of all, bodies dropping to a ghastly death on the concrete below. He died one minute before 10 AM, when the collapse of the South Tower next door hurled flying debris, striking him in the head as he was assisting fleeing office workers. His was the first body carried out of the World Trade Center. Fire Department chaplains were never expected to actually go close to the fire; remaining safely at the staging area was the norm.

But not for Fr. Mychal Judge.

Before He Was a Hero
Before he was recognized the world over as the priest being carried away by his brethren in the iconic 9/11 picture, he was a larger-than-life type of man: Franciscan priest, New Yorker, Irishman,

123

AIDS minister, recovering alcoholic, chaplain, lover of God and people. He was beloved by many; his funeral lasted two days and was attended by hundreds, from the homeless to the Clintons.

Just the day before 9/11, Fr. Mychal Judge had celebrated Mass at a dedication of a firehouse. In retrospect, many of his friends considered his homily to be an unknowing farewell: "Keep supporting each other. Be kind to each other. Love each other.... We love the job. We all do. What a blessing that is—a difficult, difficult job, and God calls you to it and indeed he gives you a love for it so that a difficult job will be well done."[1]

The Scrapper
Known as the "people's priest," Fr. Mychal Judge knew, loved, and ministered to thousands of New Yorkers. Born Robert Emmett Judge to Irish immigrant parents in Brooklyn in 1933, he was a New Yorker through and through. He had a twin sister, Dympna, and an older sister, Erin. When Judge was six years old, his father died. The young Robert assumed the role of man of the house by doing odd jobs like shining shoes at Penn Station to supplement his family's meager income. Growing up poor made living with the vow of poverty much easier for him later in life.

Had he not shined shoes as a boy, his life could have been entirely different. He attended Mass at the nearby church of St. Francis of Assisi and became friendly with the Franciscan friars there. Although young, he began to discern a vocation to the priesthood and religious life. At age fifteen, he entered the Franciscan St. Joseph Seraphic Seminary in 1948.

While not academically inclined, the young Robert Judge was extroverted and personable, fitting in well with the other seminarians. He also had a problem with stuttering, which was corrected through speech therapy.

The Franciscan

Received into the Franciscans in 1954, he was now Michael Judge. Later he changed the spelling of "Michael" to "Mychal" to distinguish himself from the many Michaels in his community. He professed final vows in 1958 and was ordained to the priesthood at Mount St. Sepulcher Shrine at the Franciscan monastery in 1961. After years of preparation, his pastoral life was about to begin.

His was a "sacramental priesthood." Like the English mystic Caryll Houselander, Mychal Judge was aware of the healing grace of the sacraments; in a sense, his whole life was a sacrament, with grace flowing from him to those to whom he ministered. His was the presence of Christ in the world, bringing healing, love, mercy, and reconciliation to his parishioners.

Mychal Judge was a fine parish priest. His first assignment was from 1967 to 1969 at Sacred Heart parish in Rochelle Park, New Jersey. The late 1960s were a watershed in America in many ways, one of which was civil rights. Racial tensions ran high in Rochelle Park after a black family moved into the all-white neighborhood. Mychal took the unpopular stance of supporting the family's right to live in Rochelle Park. Soon after this, he was transferred out of Sacred Heart parish.

An incident in his next parish, St. Joseph in East Rutherford, New Jersey, foreshadowed the courage he was later to exhibit on September 11. A troubled man in the parish had taken his wife and children hostage. Judge rushed to the scene. When his friend Fr. Michael Duffy arrived, Mychal was at the top of a ladder, successfully persuading the man to put down his gun and surrender. He promised the man that he would remain in his life and support him, a promise he kept. Later he conceded that, while he had indeed been afraid while up on that ladder, his prayer and trust in God got him through.

It was on his next assignment that he took the first step to confront his addiction to alcohol, a struggle since he was a teenager. He was appointed assistant to the president of Siena College in New York. He would often make excuses to the other friars and sneak out to a local bar to drink. It reached the point where it became impossible for him to sleep without consuming a large amount of alcohol. Sensing he was in trouble, Mychal attended an Alcoholics Anonymous meeting one Saturday evening. That same night, one of the college students was struck by a car and killed. Mychal had to inform the family. He later told a friend that, had he followed his normal routine of being drunk on a Saturday night, he could never have handled such a difficult task.

Alcoholism

Alcoholism is a complex disease, involving heredity, emotional factors, and most importantly, the makeup of the brain. In addition to being a physical and mental disease, it is also a spiritual one. The Twelve Steps of Alcoholics Anonymous, or AA, encourage trust in God, knowledge of self, and a prayer life. AA members encourage and support one another; attending meetings to receive that support is vital to staying sober. For the rest of his life, no matter where he traveled: Northern Ireland, France, Washington, D.C., Mychal always attended AA meetings.

Sabbatical

Priests and religious take sabbaticals in order to have a time apart for renewal, prayer, and relaxation. In 1984, at age fifty-two, Mychal Judge chose to go to the Franciscan International Study Centre in Canterbury, England, to continue his inner journey of self-discovery and to immerse himself in Franciscanism. The sabbatical year was a turning point in his life, allowing him to inte-

grate his sobriety into his Franciscan identity. His natural extrover-
sion drew people to him; his keen pastoral sense drew him to anyone who was hurting in any way.

Mychal later described his sabbatical year in England as exciting
and challenging. His presence at the Centre also challenged some
of the older Franciscans who lived there. Wearing jeans and pulling
his hair back in a ponytail, he exuded freedom from constraints of
any sort. Celebrating Mass, he would sometimes digress and
include his own prayers. This, along with hosting the Franciscan
Centre's first AA meeting, did not endear him to some of his peers.

AIDS

A virulent disease had been brewing in the United States while
Mychal was on sabbatical in England. By July, 1982, over four
hundred cases of the disease were reported to the Centers for
Disease Control. Puzzled, medical scientists called the new disease
"acquired immunodeficiency syndrome," or AIDS. It was especially prevalent among gay men.

New York City's gay community was the epicenter of the AIDS
epidemic. In its early stages, when the precise method of transmis-
sion was unknown, intense fear surrounded the condition. Dentists
and doctors refused to treat people with AIDS; hospital personnel
would not enter their rooms. This all-too-pervasive fear included
priests, many of whom refused to make pastoral visits or adminis-
ter sacraments to AIDS patients.

This was the situation to which Mychal Judge brought his
intense pastoral sense and energy: Upon his return from England,
he began what he called St. Francis AIDS ministry.[2] The St. Francis
AIDS ministry was an organized effort of outreach and care for
AIDS patients.

Mychal was an ideal minister to people with AIDS. More than just visit, he anointed them, brought them teddy bears, and offered spiritual consolation. His efforts were a healing balm for so many who had experienced nothing but rejection since their diagnosis. Mychal's AIDS ministry was straight out of the Franciscan tradition, recalling the legend of St. Francis leaping from his horse to kiss a leper.

In these early days of the AIDS epidemic, it was difficult to find a priest who was willing to offer the funeral liturgy for someone who had died from AIDS. Mychal stepped into this breach also, celebrating funeral after funeral. One especially memorable event was a memorial Mass for a family that had already lost two sons, with a third diagnosed with the disease. Debi Rabbene, their sister, searched in vain for a priest to say a memorial Mass for her brothers. Then she heard about Fr. Mychal Judge: "It was like we had always known him. He had such empathy for all of us and was so in tune…. After the Mass, he comforted my mother and then went over to my brother John. After that day, John was at ease with his illness and felt he could go on."[3]

Fr. Mychal Judge's ministry with people with AIDS and their families brought healing to them in many ways. After the memorial Mass Debi commented, "I was losing my faith, not in God, but in the church, because it wasn't there when I needed it. Mychal Judge did not make my faith in God stronger, but he made me believe in the Catholic Church more. He inspired me to minister."[4]

From his own struggles with alcoholism and his experiencing of the vast network of support he found in AA, Mychal Judge knew the healing value of simply being present to another's pain. Fr. John McNeill, s.j.·, another AIDS minister and advocate, described Mychal's approach: "He used to put it to me, if you descend into somebody else's private hell and stand there with them, it ceases to be hell.... He would go into their pain and rage and sorrow and share it with them and then both of them would be blessed by that sharing and feel God's grace and presence."[5] Much like St. Damien of Molokai, Mychal Judge intuitively knew that while he certainly could not cure people physically, he could heal their spirits by simply being fully present to them in their suffering.

Fire Ministry

Mychal fell into his final ministry almost by accident. In 1992 Fr. Julian Deakin asked Mychal to substitute for him as the fire department chaplain: All he would have to do was bless people at the scene of fires and occasionally visit injured firefighters in the hospital. Mychal agreed.

He embraced his new ministry with the same enthusiasm and pastoral sense he had always exhibited. He accompanied the firefighters as close to the fire as he could get. It soon became necessary to post a guard at the bottom of ladders so that Fr. Mychal would not climb up to deliver water to the firefighter at the top. He became very close to firefighters and their families and officiated at their weddings, baptisms, and funerals. He never hesitated to share his AIDS ministry with the firefighters, in an attempt to foster understanding about the disease.

Terror

September 11, 2001, dawned with brilliant shining sun, belying the coming horror of the terrorist attack that would sear lasting scars onto the American psyche. At 8:50 AM, Fr. Brian Carroll burst into Mychal's room announcing that a plane had just flown into the World Trade Center. Quickly changing from his habit into his fire gear, Mychal headed to the scene.

Office workers were fleeing as firefighters were running into the building and up the stairways. It was clear to the commanding officers that the fires were too intense for them to extinguish; their first priority would be rescuing people.

Acting on instinct, Mychal Judge went right into the scene of harrowing devastation: People who had jumped from floors above now lay dead on the concrete. After anointing one man, Mychal went into the lobby of the North Tower. Firefighters heard him beseeching God to make the horror stop. Mychal climbed the stalled escalator to the mezzanine to assist fleeing office workers. Then the South Tower collapsed.

Rubble, smoke, and dust filled the lobby of the North Tower. A piece of flying debris hurtling at over one hundred miles per hour struck him in the head. Shortly after, firefighters came across a lifeless body, recognizing it as Mychal's when they saw his white Roman collar. As they carefully carried his body out of the North Tower, a photographer snapped the now world-famous photograph.

Two Catholic firefighters administered impromptu last rites, doing for him what he had done for so many others. Taking advantage of the relative quiet after the collapse of the second tower, firefighters carried Mychal Judge's body to the Church of St. Peter, where it was laid before the altar and covered with a white stole. His helmet and fire chaplain badge were placed on top of the stole. Firefighters knelt before his body, many in tears.

When he got up that morning, Mychal Judge had prayed his usual morning prayer. It was a prayer uniquely appropriate to his pastoral gifts: "Lord, take me where you want me to go, let me meet who you want me to meet, tell me what to say, and keep me out of your way."[6] After anointing, consoling, praying with, and comforting others on that terrible morning, Mychal Judge himself went home to the God he deeply loved, no doubt hearing the words, "Welcome, my beloved Mychal!"

Reflection

Mychal Judge straddled two worlds: his life as a Franciscan friar and his ministry to gay men with AIDS. He did all he could to heal the wounds of rejection that persons with AIDS had experienced in society and the church. At the same time, he advocated within the church and society for understanding and respect for persons with AIDS.

I identify with this dynamic. I have one foot in two different worlds: a woman religious in the Catholic Church and an activist in the disability rights movement. When I first began representing the Metuchen diocese in New Jersey at disability professional meetings, there was a bit of astonishment that a Catholic sister was in their midst. I was also somewhat of an anomaly in church circles: few women religious were willing to accept their identity as a person with a disability, let alone advocate for disability civil rights.

I felt God inviting me to be a bridge between these two different worlds. Mychal Judge tried to soothe the wounds of rejection and hurt from the church that many with AIDS had experienced from the early days of the epidemic. I, too, try to bridge the disability community and the able-bodied community in the church. I encountered much hurt from mothers whose mentally challenged children had not been permitted to receive their First Communion, people who used wheelchairs telling tales of not being able to access their church or its facilities, and the occasional pastor who was upset because a developmentally disabled parishioner sang off-key. There was also the challenge of advocating for greater participation for disabled people in parish ministries.

Fortunately, much of this has changed. The 1978 U.S. Bishops' Pastoral on Persons with Disabilities stressed the fact that Jesus reached out continually to disabled people. The Pastoral also invited parishes to initiate disability outreach ministries in order to integrate their disabled parishioners into the mainstream of parish life. Most churches have made significant efforts to become accessible: installing ramps or elevators; removing pews to provide more legroom and wheelchair space; offering assistive listening devices for people with hearing loss; and asking disabled parishioners to serve as lectors, eucharistic ministers, greeters, and members of pastoral councils.

By giving retreats, talks, and visiting with disabled people one on one, I attempt to impart the simple good news that God sees and hears our hearts, not what we can or cannot do. We have a choice—we can let our disability bring us closer to God, or we can let it alienate us from God. Most importantly, God never leaves us. As St. Paul writes in Romans 8:38: "For I am convinced that neither death, nor life, nor angels, nor rulers, nor things present, nor things to come, nor powers, nor height, nor depth, nor anything else in all creation will be able to separate us from the love of God in Christ Jesus our Lord."

Nor illness, nor disability, nor addiction, nor grief, nor terrorism, nor poverty—none of life's challenges will ever separate us from that eternal love of Jesus Christ.

Chapter One: Hildegard of Bingen

1. Hildegard of Bingen, *Scivias*. Columba Hart and Jane Bishop, trans. (Mahwah, N.J.: Paulist, 1990), p. 60.
2. Oliver Sacks, *The Man Who Mistook His Wife for a Hat and Other Clinical Tales* (New York: HarperCollins, 1970), p. 168.
3. Hildegard of Bingen, p. 478.
4. Hildegard of Bingen, p. 255.
5. Hildegard of Bingen, p. 123.
6. Hildegard of Bingen, p. 160.
7. Hildegard of Bingen, p. 161.
8. Hildegard of Bingen, p. 61.
9. Fiona Maddocks, *Hildegard of Bingen: The Woman of Her Age* (New York: Image, 2001), p. 77.
10. Maddocks, p. 91.
11. Marcia Ramos-e-Silva, "Saint Hildegard Von Bingen (1098–1179): 'the light of her people and of her time,'" *International Journal of Dermatology*; 38(4), 1999, pp. 315–320. Available at http://www.dermato.med.br/publicacoes/artigos/sainthildegardvonbingen.html.
12. Ramos-e-Silva.
13. Maddocks, p. 151.
14. S. Sabatini, "Women, Medicine and Life in the Middle Ages (500–1500 A.D.)," *American Journal of Nephrology*, 14.4–6 (1994), p. 397.
15. Hildegard of Bingen, p. 475.

Chapter Two: St. Catherine of Siena

1. Conleth Kearns, O.P., ed. and trans., *The Life of Catherine of Siena by Raymond of Capua* (Wilmington, Del.: Michael Glazier, 1980), p. 46.
2. Kathleen Rooney, *Sisters: An Inside Look* (Winona, Minn.: St. Mary's, 2001), p. 49.
3. Kearns, p. 47.
4. Kearns, p. 51.
5. Kearns, p. 65.
6. Kearns, p. 66.
7. Kearns, p. 66.
8. Kearns, p. 58.

9. Kearns, p. 77.
10. Kearns, p. 101.
11. Kearns, p. 102.
12. Kearns, p. 150.
13. Rudolph M. Bell, *Holy Anorexia* (Chicago: University of Chicago Press, 1985), p. 2.
14. Kearns, p. 79.
15. Johannes Jorgensen, *Saint Catherine of Siena* (New York: Longmans, Green and Company, 1938), p. 236.
16. Jorgensen, p. 385.
17. Jorgensen, p. 387.
18. Catherine of Siena, *The Letters of Saint Catherine of Siena*, Suzanne Noffke, O.P., trans. (Binghamton, N.Y.: Center for Medieval and Early Renaissance Studies, 1988), p. 95.

Chapter Three: St. Joan of Arc

1. Giuseppe d'Orsi, Paolo Tinuper, "'I Heard Voices...': From semiology, a historical review, and a new hypothesis on the presumed epilepsy of Joan of Arc." *Epilepsy and Behavior 9*, 2006, pp. 152–157.
2. D'Orsi, Tinuper, pp. 152–157.
3. Marina Warner, *Joan of Arc: The Image of Female Heroism* (New York: Knopf, 1981), pp. 23–24.
4. Mary Gordon. *Joan of Arc: A Life* (New York: Viking Penguin, 2000), p. 20.
5. Gordon, p. 55.
6. Gordon, p. 28.
7. Daniel Rankin and Clare Quintal, trans., *The First Biography of Joan of Arc* (Pittsburgh: University of Pittsburgh, 1964), p. 34.
8. Polly Schoyer Brooks, *Beyond the Myth: The Story of Joan of Arc* (New York: Sandpiper, 1999), p. 113.
9. Marina Warner, *The Trial of Joan of Arc* (Berkhamsted, U.K.:, Arthur James, 1996), p. 42.
10. Warner, *Trial*, p. 56.
11. Warner, *Trial*, p. 96.
12. Warner, *Trial*, p. 118.
13. Brooks, p. 146.

Chapter Four: Venerable Henriette Delille

1. Cyprian Davis, O.S.B., *Henriette Delille: Servant of Slaves, Witness to the Poor* (New Orleans: Archdiocese of New Orleans, 2004), p. 5.

2. Audrey Marie Detiege, *Henriette Delille, Free Woman of Color: Foundress of the Sisters of the Holy Family* (New Orleans: Sisters of the Holy Family, 1976), p. 17.
3. Davis, p. 36.
4. M. Shawn Copeland, *The Subversive Power of Love* (Mahwah, N. J.: Paulist, 2007), p. 50.
5. M. Shawn Copeland, "The Prophetic Vision and Mission of Henriette Delille," *The Catholic World*, March/April 2009.
6. Mary Bernard Deggs, s.s.f., *No Cross, No Crown: Black Nuns in Nineteenth-Century New Orleans*, Virginia Meacham Gould and Charles E. Nolan, eds. (Bloomington, Ind.: Indiana University Press, 2001), p. 8.
7. Davis, pp. 39–40.
8. Detiege, p. 22.
9. Copeland, p. 17.
10. Davis, p. 27.
11. Davis, p. 51.
12. Davis, p. 1.
13. Davis, p. 78.
14. Sr. Sylvia Thibodeaux, interview with author, August 7, 2009.
15. Thibodeaux.
16. Deggs, p. 10.

Chapter Five: St. Damien of Molokai

1. Anne E. Neimark, *Damien, the Leper Priest* (New York: William Morrow, 1980), p. 51.
2. John Farrow, *Damien, the Leper* (New York: Sheed and Ward, 1937), p. 101.
3. Farrow, p. 143.
4. Farrow, p. 94.
5. Farrow, p. 120.
6. Farrow, pp. 143–144.
7. Charles J. Dutton, *The Samaritans of Molokai: The Lives of Father Damien and Brother Dutton Among the Lepers* (New York: Dodd, Mead and Company, 1932), pp. 74–75.
8. Farrow, p. 139.
9. Dutton, p. 77.
10. Farrow, p. 176.
11. Farrow, p. 192.
12. Farrow, p. 144.

Chapter Six: St. Edith Stein and St. Maximilian Kolbe
1. Maria Winowska, *The Death Camp Proved Him Real* (Kenosha, Wis.: Prow, 1971), p. 17.
2. Hilda Graef, *The Scholar and the Cross: The Life and Work of Edith Stein* (Westminster, Md.: Newman, 1955), p. 32.
3. Graef, p. 37.
4. Graef, p. 38.
5. Winowska, p. 75.
6. Cynthia Cavnar, *Meet Edith Stein: From Cloister to Concentration Camp: A Carmelite Nun Confronts the Nazis* (Cincinnati: Servant, 2002), p. 105.
7. Graef, p. 93.
8. Normandie Gaitley, "The Gift of Empathy," *Spiritual Life*, Spring 2007, pp. 41–51.
9. Gaitley, p. 45.
10. Gaitley, p. 46.
11. Cavnar, p. 138.
12. Anselm W. Romb, *Maximilian Kolbe: Authentic Franciscan* (Libertyville, Ill.: Prow/Franciscan Marytown, 1987), p. 160.
13. Romb, p. 161.
14. Cavnar, p. 145.
15. Cavnar, p. 141.
16. Cavnar, p. 148.
17. Dorothy Day, "Our Brothers, the Jews," as printed in *America*, November 9, 2009.
18. Pascal Baumstein, "Edith Stein and the Definition of Martyrdom," *Spiritual Life*, Fall 2006, pp. 174–183.

Chapter Seven: Dorothy Day
1. Robert Coles, *Dorothy Day: A Radical Devotion* (Reading, Mass.: Addison-Wesley, 1987), p. 35.
2. Coles, p. 56.
3. James Martin, *My Life with the Saints* (Chicago: Loyola, 2006) p. 215.
4. Coles, p. 67.
5. Coles, p. 73.
6. Coles, p. 75.
7. Coles, p. 73.
8. Coles, p. 112.
9. Mary Elizabeth Clark, S.S.J., interview with author, January 6, 2009.

10. Coles, p. 83.
11. Robert Ellsberg, "The Duty of Delight," *The Catholic Worker*, vol. LXXII, no. 3, pp. 2–3.
12. Ellsberg, p. 3.
13. Ellsberg, p. 3.

Chapter Eight: Blessed Mother Teresa of Calcutta
1. Brian Kolodiejchuk, *Mother Teresa: Come Be My Light: The Private Writings of the Saint of Calcutta* (New York: Doubleday, 2007), p. 40.
2. Kolodiejchuk, p. 41.
3. Kolodiejchuk, p. 92.
4. Kolodiejchuk, pp. 20–21.
5. Kolodiejchuk, p. 163.
6. Kolodiejchuk, p. 168.
7. Malcolm Muggeridge, *Something Beautiful for God* (New York: Harper and Row, 1971), p. 17.
8. Muggeridge, p. 17.
9. Kolodiejchuk, p. 214.
10. Eileen Side, interview with author, December 17, 2009.

Chapter Nine: Archbishop Oscar Romero
1. Jon Sobrino, *Archbishop Romero: Memories and Reflections*. Robert R. Barr, trans. (Maryknoll, N.Y.: Orbis, 1990), p. vii.
2. Doctrinal Bases, Medellín Conference, 3.
3. Doctrinal Bases, Medellín Conference, "Tensions Between Classes and Internal Colonialism." For more information see http://personal.stthomas.edu/gwschlabach/docs/medellin.htm.
4. James Brockman, *The Word Remains: A Life of Oscar Romero* (Maryknoll, N.Y.: Orbis, 1992), p. 39.
5. Brockman, p. 36.
6. Brockman, p. 38.
7. Oscar Romero, *A Shepherd's Diary*. Irene B. Hodgson, trans. (Cincinnati: St. Anthony Messenger Press, 1993), p. 10.
8. Brockman, p. 3.
9. Brockman, p. 9.
10. Sobrino, p. 9.
11. Sobrino, p. 8.
12. Sobrino, p. 16.
13. Sobrino, pp. 13–14.

14. Brockman, p. 173.
15. Romero, *Shepherd*, p. 403.
16. Sobrino, p. 21.
17. Romero, *Shepherd*, p. 473.
18. Sobrino, p. 25.
19. Brockman, p. 217.
20. Brockman, p. 219.

Chapter Ten: Fr. Mychal Judge
1. Michael Ford, *Father Mychal Judge: An Authentic American Hero* (Mahwah, N.J.: Paulist, 2002), p. 193.
2. Ford, p. 111.
3. Ford, p. 116.
4. Ford, p. 117.
5. Michael Daly, *The Book of Mychal: The Surprising Life and Heroic Death of Father Mychal Judge* (New York: St. Martin's, 2008), p. 90.
6. Ford, p. 18.

Baumstein, Pascal. "Edith Stein and the Definition of Martyrdom," *Spiritual Life,* Fall 2006.

Brockman, James. *The Word Remains: A Life of Oscar Romero.* Maryknoll, N.Y.: Orbis, 1992.

Brooks, Polly Schoyer. *Beyond the Myth: The Story of Joan of Arc.* New York: Sandpiper, 1999.

Catherine of Siena. *The Letters of Saint Catherine of Siena.* Suzanne Noffke, trans. Binghamton, N.Y.: Center for Medieval and Early Renaissance Studies, 1988.

Cavnar, Cynthia. *Meet Edith Stein: From Cloister to Concentration Camp: A Carmelite Nun Confronts the Nazis.* Cincinnati: Servant, 2002.

Coles, Robert. *Dorothy Day: A Radical Devotion.* Reading, Mass.: Addison-Wesley, 1987.

Copeland, M. Shawn. "The Prophetic Vision and Mission of Henriette Delille," *The Catholic World,* March/April 2009.

————. *The Subversive Power of Love: The Vision of Henriette Delille.* Mahwah, N.J.: Paulist, 2007.

Daly, Michael. *The Book of Mychal: The Surprising Life and Heroic Death of Father Mychal Judge.* New York: St. Martin's, 2008.

Davis, Cyprian, *Henriette Delille: Servant of Slaves, Witness to the Poor.* New Orleans: Archdiocese of New Orleans, 2004.

Day, Dorothy. *The Long Loneliness: The Autobiography of Dorothy Day.* Daniel Berrigan, intro. San Francisco: Harper & Row, 1981.

Deggs, Mary Bernard. *No Cross, No Crown: Black Nuns in Nineteenth-Century New Orleans.* Virginia Meacham Gould and Charles E. Nolan, eds. Bloomington, Ind.: Indiana University Press, 2001.

Detiege, Audrey Marie. *Henriette Delille, Free Woman of Color: Foundress of the Sisters of the Holy Family.* New Orleans: Sisters of the Holy Family, 1976.

D'Orsi, Giuseppe, and Paolo Tinuper. " 'I Heard Voices...': From semiology, a historical review, and a new hypothesis on the presumed epilepsy of Joan of Arc." *Epilepsy and Behavior* 9, 2006, pp. 152–157.

Dutton, Charles J. *The Samaritans of Molokai: The Lives of Father Damien and Brother Dutton Among the Lepers.* New York: Dodd, Mead and Company, 1932.

Ellsberg, Robert. "The Duty of Delight," *The Catholic Worker*, volume LXXII, no. 3, pp. 2–3.

Farrow, John. *Damien, the Leper.* New York: Sheed and Ward, 1937.

Gardner, Edmund. "St. Catherine of Siena," *The Catholic Encyclopedia.* New York: Robert Appleton, 1908.

Gaitley, Normandie. "The Gift of Empathy," *Spiritual Life*, Spring 2007.

Gordon, Mary. *Joan of Arc: A Life.* New York: Penguin, 2000.

Graef, Hilda. *The Scholar and the Cross: The Life and Work of Edith Stein.* Westminster, Md.: Newman, 1955.

Hildegard of Bingen, *Scivias.* Columba Hart and Jane Bishop, trans. Mahwah, N.J.: Paulist, 1990.

Jorgensen, Johannes. *Saint Catherine of Siena.* New York: Longmans, Green and Company, 1938.

Kolodiejchuk, Brian. *Mother Teresa: Come Be My Light: The Private Writings of the Saint of Calcutta.* New York: Doubleday, 2007.

Maddocks, Fiona. *Hildegard of Bingen: The Woman of Her Age.* New York: Image, 2001.

Martin, James. *My Life with the Saints.* Chicago: Loyola, 2006.

Medellín Conference. *Doctrinal Bases*, #3; Peace, #3 Tensions Between Classes and Internal Colonialism.

Muggeridge, Malcolm. *Something Beautiful for God: Mother Teresa of Calcutta.* New York: Harper & Row, 1971.

Rankin, Daniel and Claire Quintal, trans. *The First Biography of Joan of Arc: With the Chronicle Record of a Contemporary Account.* Pittsburgh: University of Pittsburgh Press, 1964.

Raymond of Capua, Conleth Kearns, O.P., ed. and trans. *The Life of Catherine of Siena.* Wilmington, Del.: Michael Glazier, 1980.

Romb, Anselm W. *Maximilian Kolbe: Authentic Franciscan.* Libertyville, Ill.: Prow Books/Franciscan Marytown, 1987.

Romero, Oscar. *A Shepherd's Diary.* Irene B. Hodgson, trans. Cincinnati: St. Anthony Messenger Press, 1993.

Rooney, Kathleen, S.S.J. *Sisters: An Inside Look.* Winona, Minn.: St. Mary's, 2001.

Sacks, Oliver. *The Man Who Mistook His Wife for a Hat and Other Clinical Tales.* New York: HarperCollins, 1970.

Sobrino, Jon. Robert R. Barr, trans. *Archbishop Romero: Memories and Reflections.* Maryknoll, N.Y.: Orbis, 1990.

Warner, Marina. *Joan of Arc: The Image of Female Heroism.* New York: Knopf, 1981.

Warner, Marina, intro. *The Trial of Joan of Arc*. Berkhamsted, U.K.: Arthur James, 1997.

Winowska, Maria. *The Death Camp Proved Him Real*. Kenosha, Wis.: Prow, 1971.

ABOUT THE AUTHOR

JANICE McGRANE, S.S.J., M.A., is a sister of St. Joseph from Chestnut Hill, Philadelphia. She is a spiritual director, disability activist, and environmental advocate, and she serves as board chairperson for Liberty Resources, Inc., a Center for Independent Living. One of her primary interests is the spirituality of disability. She received her master's in spirituality from Chestnut Hill College and her bachelor's in English from Penn State University.